Apostolic Religious Life in America Today

D1607958

Apostolic Religious Life in America Today *A Response to the Crisis*

Edited by Richard Gribble, C.S.C.

The Catholic University of America Press
Washington, D.C.

The paper used in this publication meets the minimum
requirements of American National Standards for Information
Science—Permanence of Paper for Printed Library Materials,
ANSI z39.48-1984.
∞

Library of Congress Cataloging-in-Publication Data
Apostolic religious life in America today : a response to the
crisis / edited by Richard Gribble.
p. cm.
Includes bibliographical references (p.   ) and index.
ISBN 978-0-8132-1865-6 (pbk. : alk. paper)   1. Monastic
and religious life—United States.   2. Vatican Council
(2nd : 1962–1965)   3. Catholic Church—United States.
I. Gribble, Richard.
BX2505.A66 2011
248.8'940973—dc22
2010053810

Contents

Part II. Religious Life and the Renewal of Love

Foreword

CARDINAL SEÁN PATRICK O'MALLEY, O.F.M., CAP.

Religious life provides a means of saying yes to Christ and to the Church. It is only in the context of the Church that religious charisms can be discerned, cultivated, and authentically lived.

The Second Vatican Council calls for all Catholics to read the signs of the times. We religious must read the signs of the times today and respond to a new generation of Catholics, who are different from the young people of twenty, thirty, or forty years ago. I frequently hear the presidents of Catholic colleges and universities share that they have never experienced such openness to the faith and the practice of life in the Church as they see in the young people of the new millennium. We cannot fail these young people in their quest to grow closer to the Lord.

I have seen firsthand that strong community life and genuine happiness with ministry makes all the difference to young people who would be open to a religious vocation. Our young adult Catholics want to be part of the Church's mission. They are drawn to the service projects and the missionary affiliations of our religious communities, as witnessed by the wonderful proliferation of "alternative spring breaks" for high school and college students, when they give of their time and effort on behalf of people in need. When these experiences are marked by faith formation, prayer, and spiritual direction, they can provide young people with a powerful motivation to consider religious life.

Religious communities that can read the signs of the times and say yes to a new generation of Catholics will have the greatest opportunity to flourish. We must be able to hear and engage constructive criticism from within our communities and the wider Church. We must not be inordinately attached to and unwilling to let go of models of ministry and life that have not succeeded. If we insist on holding on to lifestyles that are more for our gratification than the good of the Church, then we will not attract new members to our communities; we will not experience renewal.

Religious communities have a unique opportunity to welcome and minister to the new Catholics who have come to our shores. A strong sense of community is of great importance to our immigrant brothers and sisters; it is in the very fabric of their lives. We need only recognize that almost half the Catholics in the United States today between the ages of twenty and thirty are Hispanic, and that one-tenth of our priests ordained each year are Asian, mostly Vietnamese. The religious in the United States are ideally suited to nurture the piety and the traditions of our immigrant Catholics, who before long will be the leaders of our Church.

We must all recommit ourselves to the task of spreading the Catholic faith. Evangelization necessarily includes the proclamation of the social Gospel of preferential option for the poor, the Gospel of Life, and the defense of the family, which is the sanctuary of life. Consecrated life is a grace of discipleship that is born out of a deep love for Christ and the Church. Religious women and men need to be artisans of the civilization of love. We must recommit ourselves to the mission we professed. Great love and great humility will bring about a renewal, a new springtime, for religious life and for the new generation of Catholics who look to us for leadership.

Preface

Religious life in the United States in the first decade of the twenty-first century stands at a critical point for its future. Since the close of the Second Vatican Council, consecrated life in the United States has experienced profound and wide-ranging changes. These changes have resulted in a situation that the authors of this volume consider to be a crisis. The significant decline in numbers of religious priests, brothers, and sisters is only one factor in a much larger picture. The substantial and rapid changes in the life of the Church after Vatican II affected the consecrated life as well. Religious communities implemented broad experiments and changes in the form of their life. Many communities experimented with new procedures for daily living, eschewed the daily wearing of religious habits, altered traditional routines, and adopted new apostolates. Greater personal autonomy reshaped traditional community life and led to increased economic prosperity, as members adopted new directions and beliefs about how to live their vows. Together, these kinds of changes led in large measure to the point where the consecrated life finds itself today.

Vatican II is the event that separates religious life from its pre-1965 existence, but the Council itself did not generate the changes that led to the crisis. Rather, religious congregations interpreted the Council's teachings in a manner that the authors believe includes some serious flaws. In short, the idea of the "Spirit of Vatican II" was used as a rationale on both the personal and institutional levels to transform religious life in a manner that reflected the culture of the day more than it did the Council's call for an updating (*aggiornamento*) in a manner faithful to, and rooted in, 1500 years of tradition (*ressourcement*).

As a response to this situation a Symposium on Apostolic Religious Life was held at Stonehill College in North Easton, Massachusetts, on September 27, 2008. I attended the symposium and, while listening to the presentations, came to conclude that the message communicated so clearly and consistently by the presenters needed to be heard by a wider audience. Thus, the symposium became the catalyst for the preparation of this book. The essays in this volume have been organized in two categories: (1) those that define the crisis and articulate its origins and (2) those that propose, in various ways, an answer rooted in a proper understanding and living of Vatican II, centered in love. The message of these essays is clear and consistent: their authors believe that many individual religious and congregations have moved away from their roots and the teaching of the magisterium, leading in large measure to the present crisis. There is now a need, therefore, to return to the center, to re-anchor religious life in the magisterium of the post-conciliar era and to end the period of experimentation in which it has been incorrectly believed that the consecrated life can be lived on terms dictated by the individual.

These essays are published as a historic Apostolic Visitation to communities of women religious in the United States has recently been completed. Ordered in the fall of 2008 by Cardinal Franc Rodé, C.M., prefect of the Congregation for Institutes of Consecrated Life, and a contributor to this volume, with the approval of Pope Benedict XVI, the visitation was highly controversial. Speaking at the time of the visitation's call, Sister Eva-Marie Ackerman, representing Mother Mary Clare, A.S.C.J., superior general of the Apostles of the Sacred Heart of Jesus, who was appointed as apostolic visitator, emphasized how the visitation could strengthen communities of women religious in the United States: "The goal of the study is to 'look into the quality of the life' of women religious in the United States. In doing so, we hope to discover and share the vibrancy and purpose that continue to accomplish so much, as well as to understand the obstacles and challenges that inhibit those individuals and institutions, thus limiting their growth and/or re-directing their resources and outreach."[1] On the other side of the aisle, Sister Sandra Schneiders, I.H.M., rejected the visitation as a ploy to undermine the position of progressive women religious: "I don't put any credence at all in the claim that this [visitation] is friendly, transparent, [or] aimed to be helpful. It is a hostile move and the conclusions are already in. It's meant to be intimidating."[2]

This volume would not have been possible without the assistance of several people. First, my gratitude is extended to Father Mark Cregan, C.S.C., president of Stonehill College, and Sister Jeanmarie Gribaudo, C.S.J., for their idea to hold the symposium and become its spiritual driving force. I also appreciate the willingness of the presenters to have their work placed in this volume, and I thank Cardinal Seán O'Malley, O.F.M. Cap., archbishop of Boston, for his foreword. Lastly, I wish to thank Sister Tania Santander Atauchi, C.D.P., who encouraged me to go forward with this project and supported my efforts in every way.

RICHARD GRIBBLE, C.S.C.

1. Remarks of Sister Eva-Marie Ackerman, January 30, 2009, Found at http://www .apostolicvisitation.org.

2. Sandra Schneiders, I.H.M., "There Is No Going Back: U.S. Women Religious Have Given Birth to a New Form of Religious Life," *National Catholic Reporter* 45 (11) (March 20, 2009): 12, 14.

Apostolic Religious Life
in America Today

Introduction

The Challenge of Religious Life in the United States Today

RICHARD GRIBBLE, C.S.C.

Since Antony in the third century and the Cenobites a few generations later went to the desert to seek solitude with God, men and women have practiced religious life. Over the two millennia of Christianity new religious communities have arisen to meet the needs of the contemporary Church and society. The evolution of religious life allowed for greater diversity in practice. The monastic orders of the late patristic and medieval periods continued to serve a special function even as the mendicant orders of the thirteenth century met a new need. Similarly, the rise of apostolic orders during the Counter-Reformation met greater and more varied needs, while never abandoning the ideas of earlier generations. This evolutionary pattern of religious life continued through the restoration period after the French Revolution. Today, as well, men and women of faith continue to hear the call to serve God and his people in the consecrated life. While the style and methods of living the religious life have changed with the centuries, the ability of religious communities to stay focused on the charism of their founders and to maintain an abiding loyalty to the institutional Church have been anchors of stability in a constantly changing world. Clearly, religious life has been and will continue to be a significant contributor to the life and vitality of Roman Catholicism.

Contemporary Religious Life: A House Divided, A Changing Culture

While religious life had always evolved and sprouted new branches in response to the needs of the day, prior to Vatican II a general sense of unity and even uniformity was normative. Priests, brothers, and sisters, for the most part, closely followed the tradition of past generations, with the charism of the founders of their communities and the evangelical counsels as guiding principles. It is also true, however, that some religious communities experienced splits in their own ranks. The split in the early sixteenth century of the Franciscans into three separate communities, the Order of Friars Minor, the Conventuals, and the Capuchins, is one illustrative example. More recently the Sisters of Divine Providence in Peru experienced a similar split with the emergence of the Daughters of Divine Providence. Religious in individual communities certainly had various opinions on issues, both general to the Church and specific to the congregation, but the basic structure, especially for apostolic orders, of conducting their ministry under the umbrella of the institutional Church was not a significant issue. Religious men and women and their congregations were generally satisfied to meet the needs of God's people within the structures that had been defined for them.

The Church in general and religious congregations in particular evinced unity and cohesion before Vatican II. After the Council, however, differing visions of how to implement its teachings quickly emerged. The four sessions of the Council produced sixteen documents of three types in descending order of significance. Four constitutions—including documents on liturgy, revelation, the Church, and the Church in the modern world—were the Council's crowning achievement. Nine decrees—including important treatises on ecumenism and the lay apostolate—and three declarations—including the one document with a distinctively American tone, the Declaration on Religious Liberty—were also published. The net effect of these important documents was the emergence in the minds of most Roman Catholics of a new self-understanding for the Church, exemplified most significantly in the rise of collegiality, the increased role of the laity, ecumenical dialogue, and a complete updating of the liturgy, including the use of the vernacular language.

Now close to fifty years after Vatican II opened, debates continue to rage on what the Council accomplished. The theologian Timothy McCarthy posits the question: "What process did the council set in motion—was it a renewal, a reform, a reformation or a retrieval and reinterpretation of the Catholic tradition?"[1] McCarthy concedes that renewal and reform were central to the council, but the best description for him is that of theologian Robert Imbelli, who views Vatican II as retrieval and recovery of the true Catholic tradition. McCarthy goes one step further to suggest that the bishops built upon the tradition through renewal and reform of the Church.

John O'Malley, S.J., one of the ranking experts on Vatican II, has synthesized the debate in recent publications. He contrasts the "Bologna School," exemplified by the work of Giuseppe Alberigo, with the very recent thesis propounded by Cardinal Camillo Ruini and Archbishop Agostino Marchetto. Alberigo sees Vatican II as an event that yielded a change, even a rupture, from traditional norms and ways, a new beginning in the history of the Church, but one that did not replace the faith or diminish dogma. Ruini and Marchetto, on the other hand, insist on a link with the past, that the Vatican II documents "do nothing . . . but insist on their continuity with the Catholic tradition." They suggest that a new hermeneutic is necessary to reveal the true nature of the council: "The council must be interpreted in continuity with the great tradition of the church, including other councils."[2]

1 Timothy G. McCarthy, *The Catholic Tradition: The Church in the Twentieth Century*, rev. and expanded ed. (Chicago: Loyola Press, 1998), 66.
2 John W. O'Malley, S.J., "Vatican II: Did Anything Happen?" *Theological Stud-*

O'Malley, in *What Happened at Vatican II,* uses the basic concepts of *aggiornamento,* development, and *ressourcement* to explain how the Council effected change by means of style while simultaneously holding to the tradition of the Church. He offers many examples of how Vatican II adopted a teaching style different from that of the previous few centuries. The Council of Trent and Vatican I, as two examples, relied heavily upon juridical language like that used in civil legislation. These councils, and many others, issued canons of teaching and anathemas of condemned positions. Vatican II issued no canons or anathemas. Although it still employed juridical language, it relied heavily on rhetorical usage, language intended to evoke hope and inspire action. Vatican II talked about equality of persons and taught that some Church practices could change and that styles of teaching could be revised. O'Malley found these changes significant because they demonstrated two visions of Catholicism, pre- and post-Council, moving from commands to invitations, from laws to ideals, from definitions to mysteries, from threats to persuasion, from coercion to conscience, and from monologue to dialogue.[3]

The Council's perspective of openness came at a time when the counterculture of the 1960s led many people to question norms in every aspect of society, including the realm of religion. The unity of American Catholics, as exemplified by the "pay, pray, and obey" dictum of the 1950s, was shattered; "dissent" became a frequently used term in theological circles, especially in the wake of the publication of *Humanae Vitae* in 1968. Religious life followed the general trend of American Catholicism, departing from tradition politically, socially, and especially theologically. While the interval since the close of Vatican II and the "freedom days" of the 1960s is now approaching half a century, and religious life has experienced some

ies 67, no. 1 (2006): 4–5. See also Agostino Marchetto, *Il Consilio Ecumenico Vaticano II: Contrappanto per la sua Storia* (Vatican City: Liberria Editrice Vaticano, 2005); Giuseppe Alberigo, *History of Vatican II,* ed. Joseph Komonchak, 5 vols. (Maryknoll, N.Y.: Orbis, 1995–2005).

3   John W. O'Malley, S.J., *What Happened at Vatican II?* (Cambridge, Mass.: Harvard University Press, 2008), 290–313.

calmer waters, nonetheless fissures in the consecrated life are still readily apparent. In fact, some authors speak of how the polarization between conservative and progressive religious communities continues to grow.[4] There is a significant need, therefore, to explore the challenges facing religious life in the United States today and propose some answers.

Religious Life: The Landscape Today

The theological divide over interpretations of Vatican II, namely whether it was continuous or discontinuous with previous Church tradition, broadly informs the differing general perspectives on religious life in the United States today. The authors in this volume reflect a more traditional view that Vatican II should be read in continuity with previous Church tradition, using a hermeneutic of reform. They argue that the majority "progressive" view risks a kind of discontinuity, that in the process of transforming religious life to resemble so closely the life of the contemporary world that distinctive religious identity could be harmed rather than renewed or updated. Beginning immediately after Vatican II, religious began to divide more or less broadly along the lines of these two general perspectives. Now, one decade into the twenty-first century and forty-five years after the Council's conclusion, this general division seems no closer to resolution.

The progressive approach can be illustrated by certain statements made by members of the Leadership Conference of Women Religious (LCWR). Here we find a reading of *Perfectae Caritatis*, the Council's decree on the adaptation and renewal of religious life,

---

4 Writer and journalist Ann Carey suggests the polarization, especially in women's religious communities, can be easily illustrated from the tension felt between the Conference of Major Religious Superiors of Women's Institutes and the Leadership Conference of Women Religious. These two groups are almost polar opposites in their perspective on Vatican II and, consequently, their day-to-day living of religious life today. Ann Carey, *Sisters in Crisis: The Tragic Unraveling of Women's Religious Communities* (Huntington, Ind.: Our Sunday Visitor Press, 1997). Capuchin Father David Couturier in an address to the Conference of Major Superiors of Men in August 2006 concluded that polarization continues, often due to misunderstanding and inability to dialogue.

through the lens of two other formative Council documents, *Lumen Gentium* (Dogmatic Constitution on the Church) and *Gaudium et Spes* (Pastoral Constitution on the Church in the Modern World). The LCWR understood these documents to be a clarion call to move out from a monastic/apostolic mode of religious life into a world that it suggested should be embraced after centuries of rejection. Sandra Schneiders, I.H.M., a leading proponent of the progressive approach, has described religious life as entering "the conciliar vortex as a pretty impressive dinosaur, a huge, intimidating, and seemingly indestructible ecclesiastical phenomenon" that has emerged "as a songbird, much smaller, more fragile, less controlling, but perhaps in the long run more essential to a world in which beauty is more important than raw physical power."[5] Referring to the published statements of both the LCWR and the Conference of Major Superiors of Men (CMSM), Elizabeth Johnson, C.S.J., has suggested that "in the countries of the western democracies, the pattern of religious life that has prevailed for several centuries has for all practical purposes served its purpose and is passing away."[6]

Progressive religious and their communities, empowered by their interpretation of Vatican II, believe that the Council's call was for a renewal much deeper than for surface change. In *New Wineskins,* her first book that looked at religious life in the post–Vatican II era, Schneiders suggests that experience and collaboration live at the center of the renewal to which religious were called by the Council. In this regard, she has written, "Change is the stable characteristic of experience. Consequently, the reflection upon experience will be ongoing and the theoretical articulation of the structure and meaning of that experience must remain provisional."[7] In the first volume of her two-volume work exploring religious life in the third millennium, Schneiders goes further, stating that the depth of change for communities of women or men religious may take an individual or

5   Sandra Schneiders, I.H.M., *Finding the Treasure: Locating Catholic Religious Life in a New Ecclesial and Cultural Context* (Mahwah, New Jersey: Paulist Press, 2000), xxviii.
6   Quoted in Carey, *Sisters in Crisis,* 266.
7   Sandra Schneiders, I.H.M., *New Wineskins: Re-imagining Religious Life Today* (Mahwah, N.J.: Paulist Press, 1986), 4.

congregation into activities that are beyond the scope and certainly the control of traditional Catholicism. She writes, "Religious, especially women, must situate themselves in relation to feminism and other movements (for example peacemaking and ecology) that may or may not have a relationship to Catholicism but that are, in any case, not identical or co-terminus with it and definitely not under its control."[8] In a recent article she expressed the view that women religious must be courageous and continue their forward movement, noting that the institutional Church has always resisted newness and creativity in religious life. She thus concludes, "At this moment in history we are it"; there is no going back.[9]

By contrast, the authors in this volume tend to see the Council's documents and teachings as consistent with the past but presented in new, updated, and more contemporary language and terminology. Religious of this persuasion view *Perfectae Caritatis* as a call to update, especially spiritually, and to make efforts to return to the charism of their founder. David Couturier, O.F.M. Cap., suggests that this avenue was largely blocked by a virulent streak of secularism that invaded religious congregations. We religious have not realized that competitive secularism has changed our expectations, ways of speaking with others, as well as relating to others in everyday life. Society in general and religious life in particular have been pushed away from the transcendent God to the infinite desire for goods. Couturier concludes, "Religious life is not so much confused about Christ's identity and the Church's dogma as it is struggling for mission as it acts out its part in the theological and philosophical drama of a culture captivated by aggressive consumer capitalism."[10]

This basic idea has been made more concrete with respect to religious in the work of Ann Carey. In her study of women's religious communities thirty years after Vatican II, she laments the loss of significant religious traditions and symbols to secular ideas.

8   Schneiders, *Finding the Treasure: Locating Catholic Religious Life in a New Ecclesial and Cultural Context*, xxvi.
9   Schneiders, "There Is No Going Back," 14.
10   David B. Couturier, O.F.M. Cap., "Religious Life at a Crossroads," *Origins* 36 (12) (August 31, 2006): 183–84.

Speaking of religious life in the post–Vatican II era, she writes, "The majority of orders of women Religious in this country discarded most of their significant traditions and fashioned a new definition of religious life that is more descriptive of a secular institute than a religious institute."[11] Advocating those religious who sought to maintain continuity with the past, she describes how eagerness for change led to deviations far beyond what Vatican II said. She writes, "Sisters who were eager for change and determined to discard an authoritarian lifestyle gave an overly broad interpretation to the [Vatican II] documents, resulting in deviations from the renewal set forth in Church directives."[12]

The clear divide between the progressive and traditional hermeneutics of Vatican II and their lived experience for congregations of American religious raises the question of where religious congregations will go in the new millennium. David Couturier suggests that religious "are crossing the millennial divide . . . where theological mission and pragmatic politics intersect." He says the new era, one based on "international mission culture," must engage globalization with a theology of abundance, rather than one of scarcity, suspicion, competition, personal initiative, productivity, and efficiency. In essence he suggests it is time to "drop the hatchet" and move forward emphasizing the twin Catholic principles of communion and transcendent desire.[13] Certainly such a new vision, especially in a time of diminished numbers, will be a challenge, but religious today must serve as the seedbed for the future. Patricia McCann, R.S.M., suggests religious must evaluate the past half-century since Vatican II in honest ways that will require serious reflection "as well as the reimagining and restructuring in which women's communities are currently engaged."[14]

11   Carey, *Sisters in Crisis*, 12.
12   Ibid.
13   Couturier, "Religious Life at a Crossroads," 182, 184.
14   Patricia McCann, R.S.M., "Double-Crossed or Not? A Reflection on Kenneth Brigg's Study of American Sisters," *America* 195, no. 11 (October 16, 2005): 16.

Rationale and Contents for This Volume

The progressive/conservative divide in religious communities in the United States has been the subject of scholarly books and articles for at least one full generation. Most of that scholarship arises from the progressive hermeneutic. This is somewhat understandable when one sees that the majority of both secular and religious writers advocate the new progressive stance. The essays in this volume are one attempt to propose a different solution, one that has been obscured for far too long. The solution proposed is basically twofold: First, religious must better understand and live the teachings of Vatican II, and turn from interpretations that have in effect blurred the distinctive identity of religious life. Second, the unity that consecrated life must seek will be found in a return to the authority of the magisterium. Religious life must repair the rupture that today places the pre-conciliar and post-conciliar Churches at odds with each other. This healing can come about by negotiating four significant challenges: (1) regaining the signs of religious life, (2) understanding and living Vatican II, (3) reengaging the evangelical counsels, and (4) viewing religious life as lifelong formation in love.

The essays in this volume are divided into two sections: part I, "Present Situation and the Challenge of Renewal," and part II, "Religious Life and the Renewal of Love." The five articles that constitute the first part describe the present divergent situation of religious life, its causes, and the challenges that this environment presents to religious communities, their individual members, and the Church universal. Cardinal Franc Rodé, C.M., forthrightly describes the present rough landscape of religious life in the United States as manifested in the attrition of religious, closing of corporate apostolates, and amalgamation of provinces. Rodé bases his essay on Pope Benedict XVI's analysis of the two opposing "hermeneutics" of the Council: a hermeneutic of rupture and a hermeneutic of continuity, each with its characteristics and consequences. He explains the nature of the hermeneutic of rupture and the "spirit of the Council" it created. He examines in some detail the way in which this understanding was and continues to be applied to the Council's statements on religious life, describing its deleterious but all-too-familiar consequences for religious life today. In the final section of his essay, Rodé points the way forward by offering authenticity, fidelity, and continuity as key elements for following the narrow way of the Gospel.

Sara Butler, M.S.B.T., speaks of religious life as a great treasure that is likely to be lost unless apostolic religious successfully negotiate certain challenges to their identity and develop a stronger relationship of communion with the hierarchy. She regards it is as a "cause of scandal, a countersign" that polarization and division in the Church at large exist among and within many religious congregations, diocesan clergy, and even bishops. She addresses the theological dimensions of the current crisis and raises critical questions about certain contemporary views of the "prophetic vocation" of religious vis-à-vis the "institutional Church." Butler invites apostolic religious to reclaim the treasure of religious life by a fresh study of the documents of the magisterium and a renewed commitment to their founding charism by negotiating three significant challenges from the Council: to clarify the distinctive nature of religious vocation, to discover appropriate adaptation of the common life, and to expand apostolic concerns toward social justice. For Butler, however, an unexpected fourth challenge, the advent of theological pluralism and public dissent from Church teaching, has created competing ecclesiologies. She concludes by stating that the treasure of religious life can be reclaimed by addressing these challenges with fresh vigor and determination.

Elizabeth McDonough, O.P., by centering her discussion on *Perfectae Caritatis,* presents four areas wherein mistakes by the Curia and by religious themselves regarding conciliar documents resulted in significant errors in understanding and implementing the Council's comprehensive mandate for renewal. She first describes the historical context of social upheaval, experienced worldwide in the 1960s, that placed the Council's teaching in a tumultuous context from the outset. Next, she describes the challenges presented by *Perfectae Caritatis* and the failure to implement them properly. Thirdly, she makes a strong argument that many theologians misinterpreted, in a theologically significant way, the reordering of the vows in *Lumen Gentium* from poverty-chastity-obedience to chastity-poverty-obedience. Lastly, she suggests that the Curia and the bishops did not exercise proper and legitimate oversight regarding the sweeping changes women's religious communities were making. She refers to this loss of witness of religious life in the United States as "a personal and ecclesial tragedy of immense proportion."

The fourth essay in this first section, by Joseph T. Lienhard, S.J. speaks of the importance of signs and how they have played and continue to play an integral role in religious life. In a series of ten brief reflections on signs, symbols, and their meanings, Lienhard laments that the loss of many signs has created a situation with highly problematic ramifications for religious life in the United States today, although some of those signs have been replaced. The almost wholesale and unprecedented abandonment of accepted signs after Vatican II has helped send the consecrated life into its present malaise and tailspin. In some cases, when old signs were abandoned new ones were taken on, but these new signs often conflicted with the old, leading to a turn to secularity, conflict, and disunity. Lienhard concludes by stating emphatically that it is impossible to live religious life without signs and symbols.

Bishop Robert Morlino, in the last essay of the first section, suggests that the language of discontinuity and rupture has been so deeply ingrained in the fabric of religious life that in order to hear the message of Pope John Paul II and Pope Benedict XVI, it is necessary to unlearn what has been recently taught. He suggests that the new language necessary to right the ship of the consecrated life is centered in the vow of obedience, with poverty and chastity as derivatives of the former. He suggests that obedience, poverty, and chastity were deconstructed after the Council. As a result, the eschatological witness of religious life was transformed into a theology that extols liberation. He concludes by saying that forgiveness and greater unity can be achieved through the enhancement of the formation and education of religious.

In part II, "Religious Life and Renewal of Love," there appear three essays that collectively offer love, as understood in different contexts, as the basic solution for the divisions and disarray described by the essays in part I. In the first essay, Gill Goulding, C.J., drawing on the work of Hans Urs von Balthasar, S.J., suggests that it is our being rooted in the love of the Trinity that alone makes religious credible. It is God's love at work within apostolic religious life when religious live out their vocations in contemplation and action. Concretely this means that God chose religious, through their creation, redemption, and vocation. Additionally, it means that the self-emptying love of God, made known in the self-surrender and obedience of Christ, is at the heart of the vows of poverty, chastity, and obedience when lovingly lived. Lastly, the pattern of divine love, one of Cross and Resurrection, is replicated in the life of religious who live an ongoing conversion. She concludes that it is the "joyful fidelity of apostolic religious that bears witness to the faithfulness of God; it is divine love flowing in us and through all our apostolic efforts that gives real credibility."

Kurt Pritzl, O.P., in his essay says that perfect charity or complete love must be the engine that drives religious to find answers to the challenges that the renewal of the consecrated life places before the world. Such renewal must be both ongoing and specific to group and time. He centers his analysis and discussion, by both time and theme, within the boundaries of *Perfectae Caritatis* and *Vita Consecrata* (Apostolic Exhortation of John Paul II on the Consecrated Life and on Its Mission in the Church and in the World). The fires of renewal can be ignited by emphasizing two essential points. First, Pritzl offers the centrality of the evangelical counsels for renewal. Secondly, this renewal will be found by reclaiming the original charism of the community and its founder. He concludes by stating that the basic structures of religious life, including ideas absolutely essential to it and necessary, can be "denigrated if not corrupted" if they are not practiced in the spirit of love.

Hugh Cleary, C.S.C., concludes this section and this volume with an essay that suggests that the love needed to find a solution to the disarray of contemporary religious life can be found in one's daily encounter with Christ and is manifested in how we treat one another. Religious life lives this special love through the evangelical counsels. In essence, he states that the consecrated life itself is "the treasure beyond all price" of God's love. Using the work of Benedict XVI and Blessed Basile Moreau, founder of the Congregation of Holy Cross, Cleary proclaims that consecrated life is an imperfect sign of Christ's self-giving and forgiving love. The great challenge for religious is to move away from the self-centered life so rampant in today's society and, as a countersign, take the risk of choosing a more outward love that is self-forgetting. A proper understanding and living of the evangelical counsels can help religious to abandon selfishness and point their efforts outward toward those they serve in various apostolic ministries.

Conclusion

At the dawn of the third millennium the landscape of religious life in the United States remains fractured, but there is cause for hope. The differing perspectives on Vatican II have in some ways placed religious communities on opposite sides of a divide. Like two opposing teams they seem to battle over the playing field, sparring as they go, winning some victories and suffering some defeats. In the literature, the hermeneutic of rupture seems to have prevailed. It is hoped that this book, in bringing to the fore voices that support the hermeneutic of continuity, can be a vehicle to advance the dialogue between groups who, in the end, must work for the same ultimate goal, giving faithful witness to Christ in service to humanity, that all might be saved. It is hoped also that apostolic religious of good faith, in the love for the Church that they share, can find common ground that will aid their efforts to serve others as Jesus commanded his apostles to do at the Last Supper. May those who read this volume be so inspired to follow the lead of the Lord in all they do and say.

Part I. Present Situation and the
Challenge of Renewal

One

Reforming Religious Life with the Right Hermeneutic

CARDINAL FRANC RODÉ, C.M.

Apostolic religious life is indeed an important topic in today's Church. As a member of the Vincentian order the consecrated life has been integral to my vocation from the outset. As the Prefect of the Congregation for Institutes of Consecrated Life and Societies of Apostolic Life the care, maintenance, and promotion of religious life is the direct focus of my present ministry in the Church. As one who experienced the adventure and the turmoil of renewal in consecrated life prompted by the Second Vatican Council, the opinions in this essay express past and present challenges, but always with immense hope for the future.

The Lessons from History about Consecrated Life

Consecrated life within the Church and within civil society has never played a secondary or minor role. As Pope John Paul II wrote:

Its universal presence and the evangelical nature of its witness are clear evidence—if any were needed—that the consecrated life *is not something isolated and marginal*, but a reality which affects the whole Church. . . . In effect, *the consecrated life is at the very heart of the Church* as a decisive element for her mission, since it "manifests the inner nature of the Christian calling and the striving of the whole Church as Bride toward union with her one Spouse." . . . It is an intimate part of her life, her holiness and her mission.[1]

One can hardly overestimate the importance of consecrated life for the good of the Church and of humanity at large. From the birth of Christianity, some men and women were moved by the Spirit to devote their entire lives to imitating Christ more closely. Their consecration gradually took on the multiple forms we are familiar with today—rules and ways of life that at once express and give continuity to the charisms given by the Spirit.

Even a sketchy overview of history can show abundant evidence that without the presence and activity of monks and nuns, religious women and men, despite their acknowledged cultural and historical limitations, the history of Western civilization and the evangelization of vast areas of the globe would be immensely poorer. The history of the Church in the United States of America (as well) is rich with the contributions of consecrated men and women who have left an indelible mark on the culture.

During Pope Benedict's visit to the United States in April 2008, he addressed young people gathered at New York's St. Joseph Seminary. The Holy Father said in part: "Charisms are bestowed by the Holy Spirit, who inspires founders and foundresses, and shapes congregations with a subsequent spiritual heritage. The wondrous array of charisms proper to each religious institute is an extraordinary spiritual treasury. Indeed, the history of the Church is perhaps most beautifully portrayed through the history of her schools of spirituality, most of which stem from the saintly lives of founders and foundresses."[2]

---

1   John Paul II, *Vita Consecrata,* Post-Synodal Apostolic Exhortation on the Consecrated Life and Its Mission in the Church and in the World, n. 3 (emphasis added).
2   Benedict XVI, "Address to Young People and Seminarians at Saint Joseph Seminary," Yonkers, New York, April 19, 2008.

The first four figures Benedict XVI proposed to the youth and seminarians at Dunwoodie as exemplary testimonies of the Gospel in the United States, were consecrated: Saint Elizabeth Ann Seton, Saint Frances Xavier Cabrini, Saint John Neumann, and Blessed Kateri Tekakwitha, who in 1679 made a vow of chastity as an expression of consecrated virginity.

Some of the most epic pages in the history of missions were written in this blessed land by the heroic French missionary Jesuits who were martyred in what is now New York State and Ontario, Canada, and by the Franciscans and other missionaries in the South and the West Coast of the United States. It is significant that in the National Statuary Hall in the United States Capitol, various states are represented by religious, such as Mother Joseph of the Sisters of Providence, Saint Damien of Molokai, Father Eusebio Kino, Father Jacques Marquette, and Blessed Father Junípero Serra.

In the last two centuries, many religious in the United States have made education their highest priority—an undertaking that, as Pope Benedict pointed out in his recent address to Catholic educators in Washington, came at the cost of great sacrifice. He noted:

> Towering figures, like Saint Elizabeth Ann Seton and other founders and foundresses, with great tenacity and foresight laid the foundations of what is today a remarkable network of parochial schools contributing to the spiritual well-being of the Church and the nation. Some, like Saint Katharine Drexel, devoted their lives to educating those whom others had neglected—in her case, African Americans and Native Americans. Countless dedicated religious sisters, brothers, and priests together with selfless parents have, through Catholic schools, helped generations of immigrants to rise from poverty and take their place in mainstream society.[3]

In the last forty years, the Church has undergone one of her greatest crises of all times. We all know that the dramatic situation of consecrated life has not been marginal in this state of affairs. In practically all Western countries, observers note that most religious

---

3   Benedict XVI, "Address to the Catholic Educators at Conference Hall of the Catholic University of America in Washington, D.C.," April 17, 2008.

communities are entering the end-game of a prolonged crisis whose outcome, they say, is already determined by the statistics.

In many of these Western countries, religious have lost hope. They are resigned to the loss of vitality, of significance, of joy, of attractiveness, of life. But America is different. The vitality, creativity, and exuberance that mark the thriving culture of the United States are reflected in Christian life and also in consecrated life. Just think: since the Second Vatican Council, more than a hundred new religious communities have sprung up in this fertile soil. This is the country that Pope Benedict visited in April 2008 in order to bring the message of the hope of Christ. But when he returned to Rome, he said, "I discovered a tremendous vitality and a decisive will to live and to witness to the faith in Jesus." With great joy, he confessed that he himself "was confirmed in hope by American Catholics."[4]

The Present State of Religious Life

Despite this past greatness and present vitality, all is not well with religious life in America. The sheer decline in the numbers of consecrated men and women, the abandoning of many corporate apostolates and ministries, the closing of communities, the invisibility of corporate witness to consecrated life, amalgamations of provinces, mergers of different institutes, the graying of religious, the death of entire congregations—these realities are all familiar to us.

Under the umbrella of "consecrated life" and behind the statistics there lies a variety of situations. First, there are many new communities, some better known than others, many of which are thriving and whose individual statistics are the reverse of the general trends. Second, we have older communities that have taken action to preserve and reform genuine religious life in their own charism; they are also in a growth mode, contrary to the general trend, and their median age is lower than the overall average for religious. Neither of these two groups sees "the writing on the wall" in the sense that observers of the general trends use it; on the contrary, the future looks

---

4   Benedict XVI, Regina Caeli address, April 27, 2008.

promising if they continue to be what they are and as they are. Third, there are those who accept the present situation of decline as, in their words, the sign of the Spirit on the Church, a sign of a new direction to be followed. Among this group there are those who have simply acquiesced to the disappearance of religious life or at least of their community, and seek to do so in the most peaceful manner possible, thanking God for past benefits. Then, we must admit too, there are those who have opted for ways that take them outside communion with Christ in the Catholic Church, although they themselves may have opted to "stay" in the Church physically. These may be individuals or groups in institutes that have a different view, or they may be entire communities. Finally, I would distinguish those who fervently believe in their own personal vocation and the charism of their community, and are seeking ways to reverse the trend. In other words, how do we achieve authentic renewal? These may be whole institutes, or individuals, pockets of individuals, or even communities within institutes.

This essay is directed principally toward this last group, to offer them encouragement and ideas as they seek a way forward. It may also be of use to the first two groups, lest they lose what they have, according to St. Paul's advice to the Corinthians: "Whoever thinks he is standing secure should take care not to fall" (1 Cor 10:12).

Indeed, the recent instruction from the Congregation for Institutes of Consecrated Life and Societies of Apostolic Life on "The Service of Authority and Obedience" (May 2008) forcefully states, "Persons in authority are called to keep the charism of their own religious family alive. The exercise of authority also includes putting oneself at the service of the proper charism of the institute to which one belongs, keeping it carefully and making it real in the local community and in the province or the entire institute."[5]

To that end, it will be helpful to examine the roots of the crisis. In this way we come face-to-face with a necessary and brutal question: Wasn't "renewal" precisely what we did after the Council?

5 Congregation for Institutes of Consecrated Life and Societies of Apostolic Life, "The Service of Authority and Obedience," May 11, 2008, paragraph 13e.

Wasn't this going to bring us into a new era? And was it not precisely this "renewal" that has landed us where we are today?

First, a word on the concept of reform itself. Cardinal Avery Dulles wrote in an insightful essay in 2003:

> To reform is to give new and better form to a preexistent reality, while preserving the essentials. Unlike *innovation*, reform implies organic continuity; it does not add something foreign or extrinsic. Unlike *revolution or transformation*, reform respects and retains the substance that was previously there. Unlike *development*, it implies that something has gone wrong and needs to be corrected. The point of departure for reform is always an idea or institution that is affirmed but considered to have been imperfectly or defectively realized. The goal is to make persons or institutions more faithful to an ideal already accepted.[6]

Reform, therefore, entails identifying three basic elements: (1) something essential to preserve, (2) some way of dealing with what is essential that has gone wrong and needs correction, and (3) a new way of dealing with what is essential that has to be implemented.

The Hermeneutic of Discontinuity and Rupture

The Council, in fact, offered clear and abundant guidelines for the needed reform of consecrated life. The crucial question is: how were those guidelines interpreted and applied? Overall, the Council in general was interpreted and applied in two very different, opposing ways that we must look at more closely if we are to understand what has happened and map out a course to follow toward the future.

Pope Benedict, in an important speech in 2005, posed this question: "Why has the implementation of the Council, in large parts of the Church and concretely in religious life, been so difficult and the source of so much turmoil?" The answer he offers is deep and crystal-clear: "It all depends on the correct interpretation of the Council or—

---

6 Avery Cardinal Dulles. "True and False Reform," *First Things* 135 (August/September 2003): 15 (emphasis added).

as we would say today—on its proper hermeneutics, the correct key to its interpretation and application."

He continues:

> The problems in its implementation arose from the fact that two contrary hermeneutics came face to face and clashed. One caused confusion; the other, silently but more and more visibly, bore and continues to bear fruit.
>
> On the one hand, there is an interpretation that I would call a "hermeneutic of discontinuity and rupture"; it has frequently availed itself of the sympathies of the mass media, and also one trend of modern theology. On the other, there is the "hermeneutic of reform," of renewal in the continuity of the one subject-Church which the Lord has given to us.[7]

The "Hermeneutic of Discontinuity and Rupture" Described

The Holy Father described this false perception of Vatican II in this same 2005 speech. He said that the hermeneutic of discontinuity is based upon a false concept of the Church and hence of the Council, as if the former were from man alone and the latter a sort of Constituent Assembly. The call to change would be the true "spirit of the Council," to such a degree that whatever in its documents reconfirms the past can be safely said to be the fruit of compromise and therefore to be legitimately forsaken in favor of the Council's "spirit." This spirit that all is new and has to be made new gives rise to the fervid excitement of the explorer, the prospect of stepping courageously beyond the letter of the Council. But the call is so vague that one is immediately left anchorless, a victim of his every whim and rejecting all correction. It is idealistic in so far as it underestimates the frailty of human nature, and it is simplistic in thinking that a "Yes" to the modern era will solve all tensions and create harmony.[8]

---

7 Benedict XVI, "Christmas Greetings to the Members of the Roman Curia and Prelature," December 22, 2005.

8 "The hermeneutic of discontinuity risks ending in a split between the pre-conciliar

Given these premises, and given also the best of intentions, what calming influence could there be on experimentation, and what principle was there to moderate the tendency to incorporate into religious life the fads and patterns of modern culture?

How This Hermeneutic of Rupture Has Dominated Attempts of Renewal in Religious Life

There is a fine balance in the Council's documents, but at the time, given that the mandate was for updating, it was easier to justify change than to defend continuity. *Perfectae Caritatis* (paragraph 2)

Church and the post-conciliar Church. It asserts that the texts of the Council as such do not yet express the true spirit of the Council. It claims that they are the result of compromises in which, to reach unanimity, it was found necessary to keep and reconfirm many old things that are now pointless. However, the true spirit of the Council is not to be found in these compromises but instead in the impulses toward the new that are contained in the texts.

"These innovations alone were supposed to represent the true spirit of the Council, and starting from and in conformity with them, it would be possible to move ahead. Precisely because the texts would only imperfectly reflect the true spirit of the Council and its newness, it would be necessary to go courageously beyond the texts and make room for the newness in which the Council's deepest intention would be expressed, even if it were still vague.

"In a word: it would be necessary not to follow the texts of the Council but its spirit. In this way, obviously, a vast margin was left open for the question on how this spirit should subsequently be defined, and room was consequently made for every whim.

"The nature of a Council as such is therefore basically misunderstood. In this way, it is considered as a sort of constituent assembly that eliminates an old constitution and creates a new one. However, the constituent assembly needs a mandator and then confirmation by the mandator, in other words, the people the constitution must serve. The Council Fathers had no such mandate and no one had ever given them one; nor could anyone have given them one because the essential constitution of the Church comes from the Lord and was given to us so that we might attain eternal life and, starting from this perspective, be able to illuminate life in time and time itself.

. . .

"Those who expected that with this fundamental 'yes' to the modern era all tensions would be dispelled and that the 'openness toward the world' accordingly achieved would transform everything into pure harmony, had underestimated the inner tensions as well as the contradictions inherent in the modern epoch.

"They had underestimated the perilous frailty of human nature which has been a threat to human progress in all the periods of history and in every historical constellation. These dangers, with the new possibilities and new power of man over matter and over himself, did not disappear but instead acquired new dimensions: a look at the history of the present day shows this clearly."

reads: "The adaptation and renewal of religious life includes both the constant return to the sources of all Christian life and to the original spirit of the institutes and their adaptation to the changed conditions of our time." Read through the hermeneutic of rupture and discontinuity, the "return to the sources of all Christian life and to the original spirit of the institutes" tended to be interpreted in light of "adaptation to the changed conditions of our time" rather than the other way around.

Perfectae Caritatis contains phrases quite familiar to religious, but only with difficulty do these same religious remember the rest of what the Council said: "Let constitutions, directories, custom books, books of prayers and ceremonies and such like be suitably reedited and, obsolete laws being suppressed, be adapted to the decrees of this sacred synod" (3); ". . . to make allowance for adequate and prudent experimentation. . . . But superiors should take counsel in an appropriate way and hear the members of the order in those things which concern the future well-being of the whole institute" (4).

As we continue reading *Perfectae Caritatis,* the numbers that follow spell out beautifully the true nature of religious life and are worthy of meditation, but despite their length and density and their appeal to spirituality, prayer, obedience, love, and so on, their fate is sealed once they are read with the hermeneutic of change. The words appear constantly: "adaptation and renewal" (8), "adapt their ancient traditions" (9), "adapt to the demands of the apostolate" (9), "adjust their way of life to modern needs" (10), "express poverty in new forms" (13). In obedience, "superiors . . . should gladly listen to their subjects" (14). "The religious habit . . . should be simple and modest, poor and at the same time becoming. In addition it must meet the requirements of health and be suited to the circumstances of time and place and to the needs of the ministry involved" (17). "Religious must be given suitable instruction . . . in the currents and attitudes of sentiments and thought prevalent in social life today" (18).

It is true that these are just a few phrases picked arbitrarily from dense paragraphs that are rich in spiritual doctrine and that emphasize above all the perennial truths of religious life. But many were led to believe that by picking them out, and focusing exclusively on them in their efforts for renewal, they were being faithful to the true "spirit" of the Council. Thus rupture and discontinuity as a point of departure become a self-fulfilling prophecy, producing, precisely, rupture and discontinuity.

Religious Life Was Not an Isolated Battleground

Aggiornamento was the term in vogue, and meaning "updating," it presupposed something to be brought up to date: it presupposed continuity. What took place was a "pseudo-aggiornamento" that was unrecognizable in Catholic terms. Operating at the root of this "pseudo-aggiornamento" was what can best be described as "naturalism." It supposed the radical centering of man on himself, the rejection of the supernatural, and operated in a climate of radical subjectivism.

Aggiornamento was manifested in multiple ways: (1) in talk about holiness that is totally divorced from fulfillment of Christ's law and the concept of grace; (2) in minimizing of sin; (3) in the acceptance of the world as it is, with no need of conversion; (4) in taking the world as the criterion according to which the Church ought to be reformed; (5) in a notion of apostolate or ministry that consists in being at ease in the world rather than changing it; (6) in rejection of authority, and especially divinely constituted authority, hence the rejection of the magisterium and all canonical and disciplinary ordering in the Church.

The Results of the Hermeneutic of Discontinuity and Rupture in Religious Life

It must be acknowledged that there certainly was much to correct in religious life, much to be improved in the formation of religious. It must also be admitted that society proposed challenges for which many religious were not prepared. In some cases, routine and crusts of outdated customs needed to be shaken off. In this sense it must be affirmed categorically that not only was the Council not mistaken in its thrust to renew religious life, but it was truly inspired by the Holy Spirit in doing so.

In May 2006 Pope Benedict addressed superiors general. In part he stated:

> In these last years, consecrated life has been re-examined with a more evangelical, ecclesial and apostolic spirit; but we cannot ignore that some concrete choices have not offered to the world the authentic and vivifying face of Christ. In fact, the secularized culture has penetrated the mind and heart of not a few consecrated persons, who understand it as a way to enter modernity and a modality of approach to the contemporary world. As a result, in addition to an undoubted thrust of generosity capable of witness and of total giving, consecrated life today knows the temptation to mediocrity, bourgeois ways and a consumerist mentality.[9]

Pope Benedict's warning was something I experienced during my early years as a priest. Toward the end of the Second Vatican Council, I was in Paris finishing my doctoral thesis on "miracles of the modernist controversy." At that time in France there was a pervasive atmosphere of enthusiasm for the Council as the press and other media presented it. However, that "picture" was flawed as it presented only a partial image of the Council, as a "victory of the liberals over the conservatives."

When I returned to my native land of Slovenia I found that the communist regime was isolating the Catholic faithful, suffocating public expression of the faith and reducing it to a merely private affair. I found a faithful people within a society shaped by the ideology of materialism. I soon realized that what I brought with me from my studies in Paris was of very little use for my pastoral work. I needed to be close to the people and to respect the traditional ways of expressing of their faith. I learned so much from the Christian faithful! They taught me to love the Church, to respect the pope and the bishops in communion with him.

The great lesson I learned from that experience was this: the religious who secularized consecrated life were not doing so for the sake of the faith of the people of God. It was not the good of God's

9   Benedict XVI, "Address to Superiors General of the Institutes of Consecrated Life and Societies of Apostolic Life," May 22, 2006.

people that they were seeking. Rather than God's will, what they were seeking was their own.

Religious life, being a gift from the Holy Spirit to the individual religious and the Church, depends especially on fidelity to its origins, to its founder, and to the particular charism. Fidelity to that charism is essential, for God blesses fidelity while he "opposes the proud" (Jas 4:6). The complete rupture of some with the past, then, goes against the nature of a religious congregation, and essentially it provokes God's rejection.

As soon as naturalism was accepted as the new way, obedience was an early casualty, for obedience without faith and trust cannot survive. Prayer, especially community prayer, and the sacramental liturgy were minimized or abandoned. Penance, asceticism, and what was referred to as "negative spirituality" became a thing of the past. Many religious were uncomfortable with wearing the habit. Social and political agitation became for them the acme of apostolic action. The New Theology shaped the understanding and the dilution of the faith. Everything became a problem for discussion. Rejecting traditional prayer, the genuine spiritual aspirations of religious sought out other more esoteric forms.

The results came swiftly in the form of an exodus of members. As a consequence, apostolates and ministries that were essential for the life of the Catholic community and its charitable outreach quickly disappeared—schools especially. Vocations quickly dried up. Even as the results began to speak for themselves, there were still those who said that things were bad because there hadn't been enough change, the project was not complete. And so the damage was further compounded.

It must further be noted that many of those responsible for the disastrous decisions and actions of those post-conciliar years later left religious life themselves. The ones who have remained faithful require immense courage to shoulder the burden of reversing the damage and rebuilding their religious families. My heart and my prayers go out to them.

The Hermeneutic of Continuity and Reform Described

The true "spirit of the Council" was described at its inauguration by Pope John XXIII when he said that the Council wishes "to transmit the doctrine, pure and integral, without any attenuation or distortion." And he continues:

> Our duty is not only to guard this precious treasure, as if we were concerned only with antiquity, but to dedicate ourselves with an earnest will and without fear to that work which our era demands of us. It is necessary that adherence to all the teaching of the Church in its entirety and preciseness be presented in faithful and perfect conformity to the authentic doctrine, which, however, should be studied and expounded through the methods of research and through the literary forms of modern thought. The substance of the ancient doctrine of the deposit of faith is one thing, and the way in which it is presented is another.[10]

These words give rise to a very different way of interpreting the Council from what has been described earlier. The hermeneutic of continuity and reform elicits a harmonious dialogue between faith and reason. Reason, enlightened by the supernatural gift of faith, adheres voluntarily and lovingly to what Pope John XXIII called "the substance of the ancient doctrine" that was revealed by Christ and rightly interpreted by the magisterium with the infallible and constant assistance of the Holy Spirit. Reason enlightened by faith will not fall into the trap of modern secularism. Authentic prophetism in the Church intends to rectify behavior, not to change the apostolic revelation. Cardinal Avery Dulles explained this point well when he wrote:

> In our day the prevailing climate of agnosticism, relativism, and subjectivism is frequently taken as having the kind of normative value that belongs by right to the word of God. We must energetically oppose reformers who contend that the Church must abandon her claims to absolute truth, must allow dissent from her own doctrines, and must

10 Pope John XXIII, "Opening Speech at Vatican II," October 11, 1962.

be governed according to the principles of liberal democracy. False reforms, I conclude, are those that fail to respect the imperatives of the Gospel and the divinely given traditions and structures of the Church, or which impair ecclesial communion and tend rather toward schism. Would-be reformers often proclaim themselves to be prophets, but show their true colors by their lack of humility, their impatience, and their disregard for the Sacred Scripture and tradition.[11]

The Application and Fruits of the Hermeneutic of Continuity and Reform

Today gratitude can be given to the Second Vatican Council, which provided clear guidelines to distinguish between the substance of the deposit of the faith and its circumstantial manifestations. Continuity with what is essential in religious life does not stifle but rather encourages reform of what is outdated, accidental, and perfectible. This is evident when we read the finely balanced criteria and guidelines for renewal in *Perfectae Caritatis,* numbers 2–18, referenced earlier in my description of the hermeneutic of rupture and discontinuity.

When these same numbers are interpreted in terms of continuity, the changes asked for are never disassociated from their roots. Those seeking continuity in renewal will notice that the Council called for a renewal that is eminently a renewal of the spirit, emphasizing the centrality of Christ as he is found in the Gospels, following him on the path envisaged by the founder through the vows (2).

Renewal is found in many aspects of religious life as seen in *Perfectae Caritatis.* It is sought in the more faithful observance of the rule and constitutions (4). It calls for a religious consecration that means not only dying to sin (baptismal vocation) but renouncing the world and living for God alone, service of the Church and fostering of all the virtues, especially humility and obedience, seeking God alone, joining contemplation to action (5). It requires the priority of loving God and nourishing one's life on Scripture and the

11   Dulles, "True and False Reform," 17.

Eucharist (6). The Council sees no dichotomy between contemplation and action; the latter springs from the former (7).

Perfectae Caritatis calls for spiritual training if members of secular institutes are to be leaven in the world (11). Chastity, poverty, obedience (12, 13, 14), are all cast in an eminently supernatural light, based on faith, hope, and love. The radicality of their implications is clearly laid out. The need for common life lived in prayer, charity, and mutual support is highlighted in number 15. Papal cloister should be maintained by nuns dedicated exclusively to the contemplative life (16). The habit should be adapted, implying it should remain (17).

A number of the better-known new religious orders and movements were already under way at the time of the Council. These invariably examined themselves in the light of the orientations issued by the Council, and were unanimously faithful to its authentic spirit as expressed in the letter of the Council. New congregations founded since then have also found the key to their own self-understanding in the Council's doctrine. Though the concept of "renewal" is not applicable to a new group, the element of continuity and the essential elements of religious life as spelled out by the Council have guided these foundations without exception. Is it mere coincidence that they are growing?

In December 2005 the Holy Father summed up the fruits of this hermeneutic as follows: "Wherever this interpretation guided the implementation of the Council, new life developed and new fruit ripened. Forty years after the Council, we can show that the positive is far greater and livelier than it appeared to be in the turbulent years around 1968. Today, we see that although the good seed developed slowly, it is nonetheless growing; and our deep gratitude for the work done by the Council is likewise growing."[12]

Seeking Renewal at This Juncture in History

The questions must be asked: Where can apostolic religious life go from here? Is there new life for religious communities in North

---

12   Benedict XVI, "Christmas Greetings."

America seeking authentic reform? It must be noted that, though the background to the problems is the same, and there are common problems and challenges faced by both men and women religious (the engineering of language, the slant toward relativism, the fading of a sense of the supernatural, in some cases doubt about the relevance and centrality of Christ), it is also true that each group faces its own particular challenges. Women religious especially need to engage critically a certain strain of feminism that is by now outmoded but that still nevertheless continues to exert much influence in certain circles.

Emphasis must, however, be focused on the common elements. If rupture and confusion are what characterize the recent difficulties in religious life, then the way forward has to be a greater seeking of continuity and clarity. Like the scribe who has been instructed in the Kingdom of Heaven, we should bring from our storeroom both the new and the old.[13]

Continuity with the Essentials—First, Our Catholic Faith

It seems superfluous to say, for one would imagine there is no discussion on this point, but we must begin a discussion of continuity with the essentials of the Catholic faith. Unfortunately, we have all sadly experienced the presence of groups or individuals who, by their own admission, have "moved beyond the Church," yet remain externally "in" the Church. Surely, such an ambivalent existence cannot bring forth fruits of joy and peace,[14] neither for themselves nor for the Church. Hopefully the Holy Spirit will give them the light to see the path to true peace and freedom, and the courage to follow it. In this vein the instruction on the Service of Authority and Obedience states:

> Persons in authority have the task of helping to keep alive the sense of faith and of ecclesial communion, in the midst of a people that recognizes and praises the wonders of God, witnessing to the joy of belong-

---

13   Cf. Mt 13:52.
14   Cf. Gal 5:22.

ing to him in the great family of the one, holy, Catholic, and apostolic Church. The task of following the Lord cannot be taken by solitary navigators but is accomplished in the bark of Peter, which survives the storms; and consecrated persons contribute a hardworking and joyful fidelity to good navigation. Persons in authority should therefore remember that "Our obedience is a believing with the Church, a thinking and speaking with the Church, serving through her."

Continuity with the Concept of Religious Life as Understood by the Church

According to the Council, "Church authority has the duty, under the inspiration of the Holy Spirit, of interpreting these evangelical counsels, of regulating their practice and finally to build on them stable forms of living."[15] Both Church authority and the tradition of the Church throughout the centuries have spelled out what the substance of consecrated life is. In May 2006 Pope Benedict put it this way: "Belonging to the Lord: this is the mission of the men and women who have chosen to follow Christ—chaste, poor and obedient—so that the world may believe and be saved."[16]

Continuity with the Charism of the Founder

Continuity with the charism of the founder is of capital importance, and a key to renew and revitalize our congregations, attract vocations, and fulfill our obligations toward the young people who eventually enter our religious families. The Council insists on this. It is essential to ensure that life in our congregations is both fully Catholic and completely in line with the charism of the founder or foundress. There can be no contradiction here, since the charism was given to the founders in the context of the Church, and it was submitted to the approval of the Church. Many congregations are making strenuous efforts in this regard.

However, some religious superiors have found that this is not

15   *Lumen Gentium,* n. 42.
16   Benedict XVI, "Address to Superiors General."

enough. They are making great efforts to revive the figure and centrality of their founder; they are renewing religious observance and life in their communities; but they say the vocations are still not coming. There are two further, very important elements to take into consideration.

The Formation of the New Generations:
The Formation Program

In the present circumstances, offering an adequate, faithful formation program is a particularly significant challenge. No individual can do it alone, no individual house can do it, sometimes not even a province. Resources are scattered; there may not be much unity or agreement as regards what the substance of formation should be. Nevertheless, this is probably the single most important element that affects the long-term renewal of our congregations and our ability to attract new vocations. Therefore, it is essential that it be addressed by all those who desire to see their institutes flourish once more.

In this regard some considerations should be the following:

A. It is worth any sacrifice to dedicate to formation the most outstanding of a congregation's members. They must be fully in communion with the Church. They must be prudent, eminently spiritual, and practical. They must love their congregation and identify with the founder's charism, have a spiritual love for their charges, be aware of the strengths and weaknesses of young people today, and have the complete support of their major superiors.

B. Postulancy and novitiate programs are easier to cater for, but the challenge is greater as regards the study of philosophy and theology, or other college careers necessary for the apostolate of the members. When it is necessary to have religious study in centers of learning outside the congregation's own, these must be chosen prudently so that the doctrine the young religious receive will be sure and in depth, and the external circumstances will allow them to live an authentic community and religious life, continuing to cultivate all areas of their formation, including the spiritual, the sacramental, and the human.

C. The new vocations should be educated in the light of the rich contributions of John Paul II and Benedict XVI as regards understanding the dignity of the human person, the nature of freedom, the nature of the religious dimension of our lives, and the need for human formation.

D. They should be imbued with love for their own founder, history, traditions, and contributions, and a healthy ambition to serve souls.

E. Fidelity to the spirit of religious life and of one's institute should not be depersonalized or static. It should rather be creative, capable of finding innovative ways to develop and apply the charism and of reaching out to the new generation of Catholics and to potential members to the institute.

Active Promotion of Vocations

Vocations are a gift from God; the initiative is completely his. Nevertheless, as is his custom, he normally uses secondary causes, and he depends on our collaboration to carry out his plans. Two different and complementary ways to promote vocations can be distinguished: one can be called *indirect* and the other *direct.* Counterintuitively, what is called indirect promotion is actually the more important of the two in the context of the Church today because all religious can engage in it, the whole body of the Church benefits from it, and without it the direct promotion of vocations remains mostly sterile.

"Indirect" promotion is everything that builds up the life of Christ in the Church, and it can be summarized in three dimensions of life: spirituality, catechesis, and apostolate or ministry. And we have to focus these three dimensions to Christian life on the *two places* that most affect the vocation to consecration: on the family and on the heart, mind, and soul of the individual young person.

Often for individual religious and their communities, the reason the seed does not bear fruit is not that the ground is rocky or otherwise bad, but that many other concerns clamor for their time and attention. More directly, today religious are engaged in and worried about many things, like Martha.[17] Committees, conferences, social justice issues, press releases, and suchlike clog calendars. But there is one thing and one thing alone that will ultimately change the world, and that is the inner transformation of the human person through contact with the grace of Christ.

Spirituality is centered not on a vague religious feeling of being right with God and neighbor and having nice experiences in prayer. Its essence is continual conversion, nourished on the sacraments, and the fulfillment of God's plan for one's life. It has an objective dimension.

Catechesis is not limited to initial instruction, but is the continued deepening in the riches of the Catholic faith that alone among all religions and all versions of Christianity provides solid and completely satisfying nourishment for the intellect as well as the soul. It is essential that catechesis go hand-in-hand with spirituality, and to be able to give a reason for one's hope, as Peter said.[18]

The third dimension is action, the external living of Christ's charity that takes one beyond the boundary of his own comfort. For the individual, this is a new experience of Christ. In prayer and the sacraments religious are transformed by their contact with Christ. In catechesis their mind is nourished, but it takes the practice of Gospel charity to enter fully into the charity of Christ, who didn't hold onto what he was,[19] but came among us to serve.[20] Through ministry in the apostolate, religious walk as if they were "in Jesus' sandals."

Using the congregation's individual charism, enriching the above with the example and experience of our founders and history, religious can all contribute to the renewal of a vigorous, authentic Christian life in all those with whom they have contact. It will be well worth their while to examine the nature and thrust of every single project they have under way, to look at the use they make of time and what occupies it, and then to take the time to cleanse and priori-

17 Cf. Lk 10:41.
19 Cf. Phil 2:6–7.

18 Cf. 1 Pt 3:15.
20 Cf. Mk 10:45.

tize. Additionally, they should also look especially at the content and quality of youth programs.

This work has been called "indirect" because it prepares the seedbed of vocations (the family) and the subject of vocations (the individual young person), to have an open and generous disposition toward God's will (spirituality), to appreciate the greatness and gift of the faith (catechesis), and to be able to sacrifice and give oneself to the call for the good of souls (apostolate). It is in the lives of individuals and families where God will normally plant the seed of a vocation.

This brings us to the next point: direct promotion. "Direct" promotion of vocations is when we set out to find and encourage those young people God is calling to religious life. It supposes that religious truly believe God is working in those souls, and, therefore, they must seek with confidence and not be disheartened if success does not come immediately. Direct promotion is done in many ways: religious can speak in schools and colleges, write, invite, offer retreats and "Come and See" programs, and so forth. This must and should continue and increase if possible, using all the means available today.

Three elements contribute to make this direct promotion effective. First: the indirect preparation mentioned above (whether it was done through an apostolate or ministry of one's own community, or another community or ecclesial movement, or in the individual's home parish). Second: what we offer must be genuine. In other words, the community life and formation to which a young person is invited must reflect the particular charism of the religious family and be in full, joyful communion with the Church. Lastly: the vocation's promoter must be equipped humanly, intellectually, and spiritually for his or her delicate task.

Conclusion

It should not surprise any religious that the road ahead is fraught with challenges and difficulties. However, we can be confident of the complete support from the Church for any honest effort to renew individual religious families along the lines of fidelity to the Church and to the founder. Much honesty, humility, courage, open-mindedness, dialogue, sacrifice, perseverance, and prayer will be needed, for as Pope Benedict has stated, "Jesus warned us that there are two ways: one is the narrow way that leads to life, the other is wide that leads to destruction" (cf. Mt 7:13–14).[21]

North Americans are justly proud of the religious and civic heritage in their continent; they are aware of the impact that life here has on the world at large. The Catholic Church, as evidenced by the receptivity of civic and social leaders to the message of Pope Benedict, is called to enrich and enlighten consciences and thus give a stable foundation to society, being a true leaven in the mass.[22] The renewal of the Church in this great country, and her ability to serve, necessarily passes through the renewal of religious life.

One of the sources of my hope is the experience I had of the power of communion with the Holy Father. In communist Slovenia, people were afraid to speak out against the regime, for fear of reprisals. One month after the election of John Paul II, I was giving a speech to the theology faculty of Ljubljana University before a crowd of 1,200 people. The theme was "Christianity in Slovenia Yesterday and Today." I surprised myself by making a radical critique of the communist regime and demanding the rights of Christians. The speech ended in a thunder of applause such as had not been heard in Slovenia for forty years.

The communist ideology commission called a hasty meeting to discuss how anybody could dare to speak out in such a way. They concluded that it must be the effect of the new pope. And they were right. John Paul gave us courage. I knew that from then on, despite the consequences, I would never be afraid to speak the truth. This incident taught me the spiritual, psychological, and pastoral value of fidelity to the Holy Father. That is why I am convinced that if religious adhere to what John Paul II taught us yesterday and what Benedict is teaching us today, we will emerge from the crisis of consecrated life into a new springtime of renewal in consecrated life in America.

21   Benedict XVI, "Christmas Greetings."
22   Cf. Mt 13:33.

Two

Apostolic Religious Life

A Public, Ecclesial Vocation

SARA BUTLER, M.S.B.T.

Religious life belongs unquestionably to the life and holiness of the Church; one could even say it is an essential expression of that holiness,[1] although it is a "charismatic" rather than a "structural" element of the Church. It is a gift by which God the Father through the Holy Spirit animates and refreshes the Church with an outpouring of grace that calls forth communities distinguished by their courageous faith, steadfast hope, and passionate love for Jesus Christ and the world he came to save. Consecrated religious have a place in the heart of the Church because, by leaving all to follow Christ, they announce with their whole lives that God has made us for himself and our hearts are restless until they rest in him.[2]

Men and women who accept the vocation to religious life make profession of the poverty, chastity, and obedience of Jesus Christ

1 *Lumen Gentium,* 44.
2 St. Augustine, *Confessions* 1,1,1.

"freely, willingly, and purely for the love of God."[3] In fact, their freedom must be assured; their vows are invalid if they have been subject to any alien pressure. Religious freely ask to be admitted to public vows in response to a deep personal experience of being loved and chosen, and in the light of a strong attraction to the charism of a particular institute. This impulse to "sell everything" to buy the field in which we have found the "treasure" (Mt 13:44) is from the Holy Spirit. If our request is accepted, we commit ourselves to observe the evangelical counsels, to live in community, and to carry out a particular mission in the name of the Church—according to the charism and constitution of our institutes.

Apostolic religious are to enrich the whole Church by the moral authority of their witness as well as by their devoted service. Religious should give vivid, corporate, public expression to their desire to follow Jesus Christ and his Gospel. It is because their witness arises from a free personal gift of self, lived according to a way of holiness approved by the Church, that it possesses moral authority—the kind of authority, in fact, that is indispensable for transmitting the faith and accomplishing the Church's mission.[4]

This essay seeks to reflect on the vocation of apostolic men and women religious. Most of these religious are aware that all is not well, that something has been lost and must be reclaimed. What is this "treasure" that needs to be reclaimed? Trying to name the "treasure" may help to identify how consecrated religious, in communion with the bishops, might contribute to the creation of the "future full of hope" (cf. Jer 29:11) that God has in mind for all. To speak of "reclaiming" it, of course, presupposes that the future stands in continuity with our past.

The problem is not only that so few are joining the ranks of religious.[5] It is also that the current polarization and division in the

3   This was formulated as a question in the final vow ceremony of my congregation, the Missionary Servants of the Most Blessed Trinity.

4   In the apostolic exhortation *Vita Consecrata* (*Origins* 25 [April 4, 1996]: 34), Pope John Paul II teaches that consecrated religious are to supply the rest of the baptized with "the incentive to make a full and loving response" to God's Word through Christian service.

5   In 1993 the Nygren-Ukeritis study (David J. Nygren, C.M., and Miriam D. Ukeritis, C.S.J., *The Future of Religious Orders in the United States: Transformation and Com-*

Church at large is found among them as well. It exists in the uneasy and even fractured relationships among apostolic institutes, within many of their institutes, and—for many—in their relationships with the diocesan clergy, the bishops, and the Holy See.[6] The reality of this polarization is more than regrettable; it is a cause of scandal, a countersign. Religious are called to be vivid, visible signs of the kingdom and to attract others to Christ and his Church by the joyful witness of their consecrated lives.

New communities of apostolic men and women religious seem able to offer this witness. They are attracting vocations, and for this the Church can rejoice. Some of the traditional institutes that made few changes or made them very gradually, and some of the younger institutes that had fewer changes to make, are likewise still welcoming new members. But many communities that were flourishing before the Council are now floundering and dying (at least in the United States), despite the evident good will and generosity of most individual religious. They have experienced a decline in numbers and a rise in median age, but there is also a malaise, an uncertainty about the future. Many are stymied by indecision.[7] They may soldier on, hoping and praying for new members, but they are unable, or perhaps simply afraid, to evaluate how their own choices and attitudes affect their situation. Some long to "reclaim the treasure," but meet with inertia or resistance from other members of their institutes and cannot get enough traction to initiate a change of direction. Others are convinced not only that apostolic religious life as we have known it *will* die, but that it *deserves* to die. They antici-

---

mitment [Westport, Conn.: Praeger, 1993]) predicted that the "window of opportunity" for reversing our rapid decline would remain open for only ten more years.

6   The Vatican Congregation that oversees religious life has had several changes of title. Today, it is called the Congregation for Institutes of Consecrated Life and Societies of Apostolic Life (CICLSAL).

7   At the 2007 Assembly of the Leadership Conference of Women Religious (LCWR), Sister Laurie Brink, O.P., pointed this out and then outlined four scenarios in "A Marginal Life: Pursuing Holiness in the 21st Century." This paper is available online at http://www .lcwr.org, under Assemblies. An abridged version of the paper, with three responses, appeared in *Horizon* 33, no. 3 (Spring 2008): 4–9. *Horizon* invited a comparable analysis of issues facing apostolic institutes of men, with two responses, making this number a useful tool for discussion.

pate a future on the margins of the "institutional Church." Some are "sojourners," already so far out on the "margins" that they expect to leave Jesus Christ and his Church behind for the sake of a new, universal spirituality.[8]

The public image of unity amidst remarkable variety, of a healthy and vigorous competition among institutes, and of steadfast loyalty to the Church's pastors and her teaching that apostolic religious used to project is long gone. Are apostolic women and men religious doomed to remain divided into factions—liberals and conservatives, women and men, ordained and non-ordained, Leadership Conference of Women Religious and Conference of Major Superiors of Women Religious?[9] Is this the best we religious can do? Is this pleasing to God?

Others have made impressive studies of the historical, cultural, and sociological dimensions of the present dilemma. This essay will focus on its theological dimensions. First, I will review three challenges all congregations of apostolic religious had to meet in view of the Council's call for the "appropriate renewal" of religious life.[10] Next I will consider a fourth, unexpected challenge that emerged after the Council, namely, a crisis of faith with respect to the origin, structure, and authority of the Church that has affected the relations between apostolic religious and the hierarchy—the so-called institutional Church. It is my contention that our "different ecclesiologies" are a major source of our malaise. Finally, I will venture some thoughts as to the nature of the "treasure" religious have lost and

8   See the document from the Pontifical Councils for Culture and for Interreligious Dialogue, *Jesus Christ: The Bearer of the Water of Life* (2003), for a Catholic critique of some Gnostic and "New Age" currents of thought that have found their way into literature promoting a "new paradigm" for religious life.

9   The Leadership Conference of Women Religious (founded in 1956 as the Council of Major Superiors of Women) and the Council of Major Superiors of Women Religious (founded in 1992 and approved by the Holy See in 1995) are the two U.S. associations authorized to represent institutes of apostolic women religious to the Holy See.

10   Many Catholics seem unaware that the Council called for "the appropriate renewal" of religious life, that the Holy See required the participation of all the members in this renewal, and that experimentation contrary to canon law was permitted. As a result, they may judge harshly what resulted from a sincere effort to comply with the Council's expectation.

identify a fifth challenge that remains to be fully met and that offers them the prospect of reclaiming that "treasure."

Three Challenges Presented by the Council

The Second Vatican Council challenged apostolic religious (1) to clarify the nature of their vocation as religious in light of the "universal call to holiness" addressed to all the baptized;[11] (2) to adapt their manner of living, praying, working, and governing themselves to meet the apostolic needs of our day;[12] and (3) to expand their apostolic concerns in view of the Church's teaching on social justice.[13] How have these three challenges affected their self-understanding as apostolic religious—persons consecrated by public vows and sent on mission in the name of the Church? How have they affected community life and the ability of religious to bear corporate witness?

The Universal Call to Holiness and the Special Vocation of Apostolic Religious

The Council's teaching on the universal call to holiness held an indirect challenge for apostolic religious. If all fully initiated Christians are called, by reason of their baptism, to imitate Jesus, poor, chaste, and obedient, and to strive for the perfection of charity according to their state of life, what is special about religious life? Some apostolic religious, troubled by this, imagined that the emphasis on the universal call to holiness diminished the value of their own vocation. They asked: if perfection can be attained in other ways of life, why make the sacrifices called for by the vows? Many others, however, embraced the new emphasis. They gladly announced their solidarity with the laity and renounced any vestiges of privilege, deliberately distancing themselves from whatever might signify "elit-

---

11 *Lumen Gentium*, 39–42 (chapter 5).

12 *Perfectae Caritatis*, 3.

13 *Gaudium et Spes* 1, 21, 27, 43, passim. The challenge was addressed principally to the Catholic laity, in view of their specific vocation "to seek the kingdom of God by engaging in temporal affairs and directing them according to God's will" (*Lumen Gentium*, 31), but many religious heard in it a stirring and profound invitation to reconsider their own mission.

ism" or imply the "superiority" of the religious vocation.[14] In their desire to repudiate "elitism," however, some abandoned not only the privileges they now disdained but also some of the ascetical disciplines and devotional practices that gave public witness to their quest for holiness of life. The effort to avoid "elitism," in fact, led some women and men religious to make adaptations that have obscured their identity as publicly consecrated, ecclesial persons, and have sometimes scandalized the laity.

So what is distinctive about the religious life? The Council teaches that the difference lies in the special call religious receive—a gift of the Holy Spirit—and in the response by which they commit themselves to the pursuit of Christian holiness under a new "title."[15] As Pope John Paul II pointed out in *Vita Consecrata*,

> all those reborn in Christ are called to live out, with the strength which is the Spirit's gift, the chastity appropriate to their state of life, obedience to God and to the Church, and a reasonable detachment from material possessions: for all are called to holiness, which consists in the perfection of love. *But Baptism in itself does not include the call to celibacy or virginity, the renunciation of possessions or obedience to a superior, in the form proper to the evangelical counsels.*[16]

The religious life, undertaken by means of the vows, presupposes "a particular gift of God not given to everyone . . . a specific gift of the Holy Spirit."[17] Religious have received a vocation to strive for holiness by means that are "over and above" what is required of all the baptized.

Much attention has been given to the meaning and "witness value" of the vows since the Council. In an effort to "accentuate the positive and eliminate the negative," some authors have proposed that the vows actually commit religious only to the practice of the

---

14   Pope John Paul II continued to insist, however, on the "superiority" of consecrated virginity over marriage. See *Familiaris Consortio,* 16 and 37; *Mulieris Dignitatem,* 22; and General Audience of April 7, 1982 (*L'Osservatore Romano,* English edition, April 19, 1982, 7ff.).

15   The new "title" would be the profession of vows or similar sacred bonds; see *Lumen Gentium,* 44 (Abbott translation), and the *Code of Canon Law,* canon 573 §1.

16   *Vita Consecrata* (1996), 30 (emphasis added).

17   Ibid.

virtues, for example, that poverty means "living simply," chastity means "loving generously," and obedience means "listening attentively for indications of God's will."[18] But one cannot vow to do what is already required! The vows are promises made to God concerning some good that is "possible and *better*" (emphasis added).[19] What is this "good"? It is the good of a covenant relationship by which one freely and publicly binds oneself to the following of "the Lord Jesus, who, virginal and poor (cf. Matthew 8:20; Luke 9:58), redeemed and sanctified [us] by obedience unto death on the cross (cf. Philippians 2:8)."[20]

While it is true that the "perfection" of the vow lies in the practice of the virtues, the vows themselves commit religious to very specific obligations that, taken together, give distinctive shape to their way of life. By the vow of chastity they oblige themselves to observe perfect continence in celibacy. By poverty, they promise to be dependent upon their religious institutes and to follow their laws about the use and disposition of goods. By obedience religious submit their wills to lawful superiors when they command in keeping with the constitutions.[21] Religious freely choose to do this out of a desire to return love for love by making a total gift of themselves to Christ. They make a serious, public commitment, on the order of marriage, and the Church, by accepting their vows, consecrates them—sets them apart—as public witnesses to the transcendent value of belonging wholly to the Lord and seeking first the coming of his kingdom.

In relation to this distinctive vocation, religious need to examine their consciences. Have we accepted one of the new "theologies" of

---

18   In 1986 Sr. Sandra M. Schneiders, I.H.M. (*New Wineskins: Re-imagining Religious Life* [Mahwah, NJ: Paulist, 1986]) proposed that the vows be understood as profession of a way of life rather than a commitment to undertake specific obligations. According to Fr. Diarmuid O'Murchu, M.S.C. (*Consecrated Religious Life: The Changing Paradigms* [Maryknoll, N.Y.: Orbis Books, 2005]) chastity may be seen as a vow for relatedness (or a commitment to erotic liberation); poverty, a vow for mutual sustainability/justice-making; and obedience, a vow for mutual collaboration.

19   Canon 1191 §1: "A vow, that is, a deliberate and free promise made to God about a possible and better good, must be fulfilled by reason of the virtue of religion."

20   *Perfectae Caritatis*, 1.

21   Canons 599–601.

religious life that empties the vows of their specific objects and obligations?[22] Have we used our desire for solidarity with the laity to excuse ourselves from the asceticism that our life requires if we are to build up the Church by the prophetic witness of holiness? Have we become so "laid back," "relaxed," and immersed in the world shaped by TV and consumerism that we no longer constitute a sign for others? Are we indistinguishable from generous laypersons whose good works are motivated by faith?

Adaptation for the Apostolate and the "Monastic" Lifestyle

Perfectae Caritatis directed that the "manner of living, praying and working" of men and women religious should be suitably adapted not only to the modern physical and psychological circumstances of the members but also, as required by the nature of each institute, to the necessities of the apostolate, the demands of culture, and social and economic circumstances.[23] This has been a tall order. For many, and in particular for women religious and lay brothers, modern circumstances seem to require the acquisition of professional credentials; greater specialization, in turn, has led to more individualized apostolates. Several interrelated factors have conspired to bring about changes in the way many apostolic religious are employed and assigned: the impact of the many departures from religious institutes; the priest "shortage" and consequent demand for religious to supply certain pastoral services; the growing "professionalization" of ministries open to the non-ordained, lay as well as religious, and the need religious now have for adequate compensation in light of their responsibility for their aged and in-

22   In an address to vocation directors, Sr. Doris Gottemoeller, R.S.M., makes this critical observation: "Unfortunately, there is a subtle tendency among some of our members to act as if the requirements of our way of life as spelled out in our constitutions are some kind of pious rhetoric. . . . Therefore the passion required to vow celibacy is diluted to 'remaining unmarried': the generosity of evangelical poverty becomes sending a regular assessment to the motherhouse; the selflessness of religious obedience is reduced to attending a few community meetings; fidelity to congregational mission means keeping a job; and the shared spiritual life of the congregation is ignored in favor of private spiritual journeys." See "Religious Life: Who Is Invited and to What?" *Origins* 26, no. 17 (October 16, 1996): 265–69.

23   *Perfectae Caritatis*, 3.

firmed members. Some of these developments are the result of their own choices; others are outside their control. In any event, the move toward professionalization has had profound consequences both for common life and for the possibility of supervising and coordinating the ministries of apostolic religious to ensure their conformity with the institute's charism.[24]

The challenge to make adaptations required by the contemporary situation in ministry led religious to consider critically the differences between an "apostolic" as compared to a "monastic" lifestyle. There were immediate and direct implications for religious whose identity as "semi-cloistered" prevented them from everyday interactions with the laity, but the choices made in this regard have ultimately affected almost all religious. During the years of experimentation, religious evaluated practices and patterns that were once assumed to characterize religious life (e.g., common life "under one roof," a set schedule or horarium, daily liturgical prayer and spiritual exercises in common, a distinctive habit, a local superior in every community). Some abandoned these elements or made them optional, on the grounds that they were vestiges of a "monastic" lifestyle no longer required of or appropriate to apostolic religious.[25] The increasing professionalization and "parochialization" of the ministries did, in fact, require the abandonment of some customs (like the prohibition of eating with the laity) and much more flexibility with respect to certain of them (like the horarium, daily Mass in common, and the religious habit).

As many have pointed out, it is high time to assess the impact these adaptations have had on the lives of religious, on the witness they hope to give, and on their ability to attract new recruits.[26] If an

24   See Sr. Patricia Wittberg, S.C., *From Piety to Professionalism, and Back? Transformation of Organized Religious Virtuosity* (Lanham, Md.: Rowman and Littlefield, 2006); also, Melanie Morey and John J. Piderit, S.J., *Catholic Higher Education: A Culture in Crisis* (Oxford: Oxford University Press, 2006), ch. 9: "Cultural Collapse and Religious Congregations of Women," 245–73.

25   St. Ignatius Loyola made similar adjustments in establishing the Jesuits. In general, religious priests have enjoyed much greater freedom to dispense with the "monastic" elements than women religious.

26   Common life, for example, has taken on heightened importance now that young

institute has abandoned elements the Holy See identifies as essential to religious life,[27] for example, one must ask whether it should plan to reclaim them, or whether the institute itself should be reclassified as belonging to some other category of consecrated life.[28]

One such element is the obligation of common life. This continues to be the subject of vigorous debate. Some favor redefining "common life" in such a way that it may be understood to include religious who live alone for the sake of their ministry but come together regularly in small groups for mutual support; others want to insist that it entails actually living together under one roof and under the direction of a local superior.[29] These debates are greatly complicated by the realities of ministry placement (e.g., the difficulties involved in arranging a corporate contract, finding ministries in the same locale, and securing housing). Some may urge that the institute's apostolic goals should take priority over common life (strictly defined), which they regard as a "monastic" value. It is not clear how this tension should be resolved, and the resolution will differ from one institute to another, but these debates should not proceed without reference to the Holy See's determination that common life belongs to the definition of religious life, including apostolic religious life—by contrast, for example, with secular institutes.[30]

Common life is prescribed not simply for reasons of convenience and economy, nor even for mutual support in ministry, but because it manifests the members' communion in Christ. By their consecration, members of a religious institute share the same traditions, spirituality, apostolic purpose, resources, and constitutions.

---

adults have the option of pursuing a career in lay ministry. It becomes one of the distinctive elements that is attractive to many of them.

27   See Sacred Congregation for Religious and Secular Institutes (SCRIS), "Essential Elements in the Church's Teaching on Religious Life as Applied to Institutes Dedicated to the Works of the Apostolate," *Origins* 13 (July 7, 1983): 18–22.

28   According to CICLSAL's "Fraternal Life in Community" (*Origins* 23, no. 40 [March 24, 1994]: 65 [e]), religious institutes in which the majority of members no longer live in community "would no longer be able to be considered true religious institutes."

29   *Essential Elements*, 2; canons 607 §2 and 608.

30   For an enumeration of these differences, see Fr. David F. O'Connor, S.T., "Two Forms of Consecrated Life: Religious and Secular Institutes," *Review for Religious* 45 (March–April 1986): 205–19.

Their sisterly or brotherly communion announces that persons who love God are able to love and sustain each other, accept one another's gifts and limitations, share joys and sorrows—despite differences in age, race, language, nationality, culture, temperament, and ministerial competence. Because the asceticism of community life demands love, forgiveness, patience, and mutual self-giving, it contributes to growth in holiness. Vowed life, in fact, has serious practical consequences chiefly for those who live together. In an age of exaggerated individualism, community life is truly a prophetic sign. By living together, even at great cost, religious are able to bear striking witness to the Trinitarian mystery of self-emptying love.

With regard to the adaptations religious have made for the sake of mission, a few questions are pertinent: Have we—out of necessity or by our own choice—abandoned elements that are, in fact, essential to religious life? Does our common residence function only as a hotel? Are we content to make "common life" optional, as a matter of practical necessity, or do we actively seek ways to live together? Are we willing to give it greater priority for the sake of attracting vocations? Given the professionalization of non-ordained ministries, is it possible to reclaim common life even if we want to do so? What factors within and outside of our control now militate against it? What might bishops, vicars for religious, and pastors do to enable and support common life for apostolic religious?

Commitment to Social Justice and the Direct Proclamation of the Gospel

A third challenge faced by most apostolic religious during the immediate post-conciliar era came from the Council's emphasis on social justice.[31] They took up the task of adaptation and renewal during the era of the civil rights movement, the War on Poverty, the Vietnam War, the second wave of the feminist movement, the Equal Rights Amendment, and liberation theology. Apostolic religious who

---

31   Pope John XXIII wrote the encyclicals *Mater et Magistra* (1961) and *Pacem in Terris* (1963). The Council produced *Gaudium et Spes* (1965), and soon afterward Pope Paul VI wrote the encyclical *Populorum Progressio* (1967), and the apostolic letter *Octogesima adveniens* (1971).

read *Gaudium et Spes* and the 1971 Synod of Bishops' document "Justice in the World" took very much to heart the assertion that "action on behalf of justice and participation in the transformation of the world fully appear . . . as a constitutive dimension of the preaching of the Gospel."[32] In this and in documents of the Holy See addressed specifically to apostolic religious,[33] they found ample support for redirecting their ministries to the relief of the poor and oppressed, and reformulating their goals to include a commitment to social justice and, more recently, to "eco-justice."

Apostolic religious have taken up this challenge with enthusiasm, eager to correct what was for some a rather exclusive preoccupation with the Church's internal life and health, to the neglect of the justice issues of the times, such as racism. A commitment to justice, peace, and the integrity of creation continues to have high priority in many apostolic institutes.[34] When religious discuss their priorities in mission they should not feel forced to choose between the commitment to social justice and the direct proclamation of the Gospel with the intention to convert individuals to Christ and bring them to sacramental life in the Catholic Church. These objectives belong together. Evangelization, in the broad sense given it by Pope Paul VI, is not limited to the conversion of individuals to Christ; it must also touch and transform cultures.[35]

Having said this, however, Pope Paul insisted, "There is no true evangelization if the name, the teaching, the life, the promises, the kingdom and the mystery of Jesus of Nazareth, the Son of God are not proclaimed."[36] More recently, Pope John Paul II called for a "new evangelization" of nominal Christians, that is, those among the baptized who live far from Christ and his Gospel.[37] The Pew Fo-

---

32 *Justitia in mundo*, 6.

33 Pope Paul VI, *Evangelica Testificatio* (1972), and SCRIS, *Religious and Human Promotion* (1978/80).

34 When religious committed to "justice issues" remain silent about abortion or become advocates for political positions contrary to Catholic teaching, however, their capacity to bear witness suffers a grievous wound that may injure their credibility over all.

35 See Paul VI, *Evangelii Nuntiandi* (1975), 18–20.

36 Ibid., 22.

37 Pope John Paul II, *Redemptoris Missio* (1990), 33.

rum of spring 2008 provided evidence that many Catholics in the U.S. no longer have a sense of living faith.[38] Several studies of young adults and reports from Catholic colleges confirm the suspicion that the Church may lose yet another generation.[39]

How should men and women religious respond? Which founders of religious communities entrusted to their members the task of educating the Church's children and youth? How can religious ensure the intellectual, moral, and spiritual formation of coming generations of Catholics? Have we stopped worrying about the eternal salvation of those we serve? The proclamation of the kingdom must include handing on the Gospel message by word and example, introducing young people to Jesus Christ, calling for conversion of heart, and leading them to full participation in the Church's life.[40]

Most apostolic religious are hard at work, in fact, doing just these things; often they are among the last members of their institutes to serve in the parish, school, hospital, or agency they once staffed. Religious are still running Catholic schools and parishes, social service agencies, and many other Catholic institutions. It is puzzling, however, that many apostolic religious focus resolutely on the world's agenda and global issues, yet give little attention to the urgent needs of the Church. Why do some religious and their national leadership conferences seem more concerned with the future of Earth than the future of the Church? If—as I would maintain—it is not a matter of "either-or" but of "both-and," what accounts for this selective emphasis? My guess is that the answer is related to the influence, direct or indirect, of the fourth, unexpected challenge, namely, contemporary theological proposals about the nature of the Church.[41]

38   "The U.S. Religious Landscape Survey," published by the Pew Forum on Religion and Public Life in April, provided disturbing evidence about major changes among U.S. Catholics. The United States Conference of Catholic Bishops took this up at their June 2008 meeting.

39   See the Center for Applied Research in the Apostolate *(CARA)* reports of the past few years, online at http://www.cara.georgetown.edu/carapr.htm.

40   Pope Benedict XVI, in the encyclicals *Deus Caritas Est* (2005) and *Spe Salvi* (2007), reminds us that faith is the source of the Church's charitable activity, and that "progress" is never cumulative because human freedom includes the possibility of sin.

41   A fuller account of the difficulties would include Christology, the doctrine of

A Fourth, Unexpected Challenge: Competing "Ecclesiologies"

The fourth challenge has been the advent of unprecedented theological pluralism and public dissent within the Catholic Church. The period of adaptation and renewal coincided with a time of trial for the whole Church in which many religious mourned the departure of friends and colleagues, debated optional celibacy, protested against *Humanae Vitae,* engaged in a succession of liturgical "experiments," and endured endless meetings. Some undertook civil disobedience on behalf of civil rights and in opposition to the Vietnam War. They then applied the lessons learned to internal congregational and ecclesial issues, spurred on by the logic of liberation theology. Many women religious, caught up in the feminist movement, claimed the right to self-determination as regards the future of their own institutes;[42] they became advocates for lay ministry, and took the lead in the movement for women's ordination. In 1983, when the revised Code of Canon Law was promulgated and the Holy See proclaimed that the period of "experimentation" had come to an end, many women and men religious showed little or no interest in dialoguing with the bishops about how they measured up to the "Essential Elements in the Church's Teaching on Religious Life," a document prepared by the Holy See as an assessment tool.

It was more than a matter of poor timing or self-assertion, however, for critical theological questions were part of the mix—questions concerning faith and morals, method and content, historical consciousness and the development of doctrine. Certain critical questions about the Church have affected apostolic religious. One such issue, mentioned earlier, was the crisis of faith with respect to

---

God, and divine revelation. See the report of the doctrine committee of the Spanish episcopal conference, "Theology and Secularization" (2006) at http://www.conferenciaepiscopal .es/documentos/Conferencia/teologia.htm.

42 Sr. Sandra Schneiders, I.H.M., in *New Wineskins,* 2, explained: "Rather than testing the validity of their experience by its conformity to the theory [as proposed by the Congregation for Religious], [women religious] have tested the validity of the theory by its adequacy to their experience."

the origin, nature, and authority of the Church, and thus of the relation of religious life to the hierarchy, "the institutional Church." Some apostolic religious have approached these questions as "justice issues," in line with this assertion from the 1971 Synod of Bishops: "While the Church is bound to give witness to justice, she recognizes that anyone who ventures to speak to people about justice must first be just in their eyes; hence, we must undertake an examination of the modes of action, of the possessions, and of the lifestyle found within the church itself."[43]

It was easy to move from protesting injustices in the social order to protesting what were alleged to be injustices in the Church: mandatory celibacy for the clergy, Pope Paul's decision (against the majority opinion) in *Humanae Vitae,* the formal disciplinary measures taken against theologians, such as Hans Küng, Leonardo Boff, Charles Curran, and the priests and religious who signed the "abortion ad" in the *New York Times,* and disciplinary measures against various men and women religious involved in politics. By 1975, the reservation of priestly ordination to men was added to the list of "justice issues." Since that time many Catholics continue to claim, on this basis, that women are unfairly barred from "full participation" in the Church. The list of alleged "injustices" has grown, and public protests continue to be forthcoming. Today, for example, the issues include claiming certain "rights" for divorced and remarried Catholics and for persons with homosexual inclinations. The revelations of clerical sexual abuse and the painfully inadequate response of bishops and major superiors of men has served to confirm the suspicions of conservatives and liberals alike that the hierarchy cannot be trusted to have the good of the people at heart.

Many apostolic religious, perhaps in response to these decisions and the bitter disappointments of the recent scandals, have adopted the views of Catholic theologians who trace our ecclesial difficulties to systemic or structural causes, in particular to the Church's hierarchical constitution. Some religious, not only popularizers but also trained theologians, propose that the prophetic vocation of women

---

43 *Justitia in mundo,* 40.

and men religious is to denounce injustices in the Church.[44] Some call for "structural change" in the Church. At first this was a way of insisting that women and married men ought to be eligible for ordination to the priesthood; ordination was seen as the route to "full participation." Many today, however, no longer seek priestly ordination because they now envision the reform of the Church as its transformation into a "discipleship of equals" that has no place for the ministerial priesthood and apostolic hierarchy.

Some leading feminist theologians publicly promote one or another version of this agenda,[45] and their opinions have influenced the thinking and attitudes of many women religious. Some male religious also lodge complaints against the hierarchy and even dispute the Church's teaching, reiterated at Vatican II, that the ministerial priesthood differs in kind (essentially) and not only in degree from the common priesthood of the faithful.[46] Dissent on whether there is an "essential difference" between the ordained and the non-ordained touches on the sacramental structure and divine constitution of the Church. This inevitably raises the question of authority in the Church.[47] Who has the right to teach and to make decisions in and for the Church—only the clergy? Should not everyone have a say in what touches everyone? Should not all members have a say about Church teaching and participate directly in decision making? Have the bishops and the pope simply arrogated to themselves an authority or power over the rest of the baptized that Jesus never intended?

Apostolic religious—theologians, publishers, social activists, major superiors—have been entertaining these critical questions, some

44   See Fr. Michael H. Crosby, O.F.M., Cap, *Can Religious Life Be Prophetic?* (New York: Crossroad, 2005).

45   Sr. Sandra M. Schneiders, I.H.M., writes: "Although the symbolic flash-point of the confrontation is the ordination of women, the actual and comprehensive object of the feminist project is the dismantling of the patriarchal system of domination and subordination that structures the institutional Church and its replacement by a system of Gospel equality, justice, and love." *Finding the Treasure: Locating Catholic Religious Life in a New Ecclesial and Cultural Context* (New York/Mahwah: Paulist Press, 2000), 355.

46   See *Lumen Gentium*, 10.

47   In a recent article in *Commonweal* 135, no. 7 (April 11, 2008), "Why Not? Scripture, History, and Women's Ordination," by Fr. Robert Egan, S.J., this logic is evident. See also my reply and his rejoinder in the July 18, 2008, issue of *Commonweal*. I acknowledge that I overstated his position in my reply.

as protagonists for change and others as protagonists for fidelity to the magisterium. These disputes have inevitably had an impact on the way religious responded to the three challenges mentioned earlier, and have divided them from one another. Even those who sincerely desire to stand fast in the "radical middle" inevitably feel the influence of these currents of thought.

Polarization: Hierarchically Structured Church versus "Discipleship of Equals"

One hears apostolic religious explain their differences by saying, "We have different ecclesiologies," and they are correct.[48] They usually claim one of two positions. On the one hand, there are the "conservatives" who accept the Church's hierarchical structure, teaching authority, and jurisdiction; they are eager to collaborate with the bishops, gain their approval, and be publicly associated with them. On the other hand, there are the "liberals" who are committed to the Church as "the People of God" but feel alienated from the "institutional Church." They are wary of distinctions based on sex or status or power, and they long for the day when all "dualistic hierarchies" are brought down and replaced by a "discipleship of equals."[49]

Apostolic religious in the second group are at odds in various degrees with the "institutional Church," that is, with the clergy, and especially the bishops, including the bishop of Rome. Some reject hierarchical authority outright because they think it represents the triumph of patriarchy ("father-rule") and is "contrary to the message of Jesus and antithetical to the Reign of God."[50] Others do not reject the hierarchy as such, but only certain of its doctrinal and disciplinary

48 I leave to one side the still deeper issue of different philosophical and theological choices, e.g., the question of "postmodernism" identified by Sr. Elizabeth A. Johnson, C.S.J., in a "white paper" she prepared at the request of LCWR, "Between the Times," *Review for Religious* 53 (January–February 1994): 6–28.

49 This expression, which is in itself quite legitimate, has been given a specific antihierarchical meaning in the work of feminist theologian Elisabeth Schüssler Fiorenza, *Discipleship of Equals: A Critical Feminist Ekklesia-logy of Liberation* (New York: Crossroad, 1993), 184–87, passim.

50 This formulation of the feminist analysis is found in Schneiders, *Finding the Treasure*, 355.

judgments or what they regard as its abusive manner of exercising authority. In the first case, apostolic religious claim to owe allegiance to the "People of God," but envision this "People" as an unstructured community of believers, devoid of hierarchical authority.[51] This "model of the Church" is incompatible with Catholic doctrine.

Although a certain kind of feminism provides the ideological foundation for this critique, it is not only women religious who publicly espouse and promote these antihierarchical options. Many who do not directly promote the critique do so indirectly by turning a deaf ear to the magisterium's teaching on religious life, moral questions, and matters of doctrine and liturgy. Some who embrace a "prophetic call" to inaugurate the "reform of church structures" assume the role of the loyal opposition vis-à-vis the hierarchy. Religious priests in clerical institutes, because they are ordained, have the capacity to develop alternative or parallel ways of "being church." Some of them exercise considerable influence through their parishes, their preaching and teaching ministries, their retreat and sabbatical programs, and their sponsorship of seminaries, universities, journals, and publishing houses.

By contrast and often in deliberate response to these developments, other women and men religious have firmly and publicly claimed their ecclesial identity, as traditionally understood. They stand as witnesses against their liberal sisters and brothers in religion.[52] The public perception of apostolic religious is that we are divided, as institutes and within many of our institutes, by our "ecclesiologies," that is, our relationship with the hierarchy. We are categorized as "true believers" or "rebels," "restorationist" or "renewed."

It must be acknowledged that many apostolic religious remain aloof from this dispute. They are the "silent majority"—men and women religious who do not want to return to pre–Vatican II patterns but are not ideologically committed to a radical program of

51 One has only to reread *Lumen Gentium* to notice that the Church is presented as, by divine institution, an internally differentiated, hierarchically structured community. Chapter 2 on the People of God is followed by chapter 3 on the Hierarchy.

52 See Fr. Benedict Groeschel, C.F.R., "The Life and Death of Religious Life," *First Things* 174 (June/July, 2007): 12–15.

Church reform, in spite of some disillusionments and setbacks. They are deeply immersed in their ministry and feel no responsibility for the state of religious life as a whole. At best, they may be troubled by the dearth of new vocations in their own institutes or worried about losing their "job" and having to find a new one. They might pick up a book about religious life on retreat and set it down as offering disturbing or alien advice, but they probably do not mention this for fear of seeming out of step. If a sister or brother instead of a priest is giving the homily at Mass, they may ask why, but they accept someone else's assurance that under some circumstances this is permitted. They may wonder why the community now prays from an alternative breviary with non-scriptural readings and an alternative doxology, but they assume someone more learned than they knows the explanation. In fact, they probably try to avoid calling each other's judgment into question in order to steer clear of controversy. Perhaps only those in leadership, vocation recruitment, or formation are paying close attention to the consequences that follow from the radical or antihierarchical ecclesiology.

The "Discipleship of Equals" Ecclesiology: Some Consequences

What are the consequences, for apostolic religious, of adopting the "discipleship of equals" ecclesiology? First, with respect to understanding the vows as a distinctive element in religious life, it must be said forthrightly that those who reject the God-given authority of the hierarchy, for whatever theological reason, simply cut the ground out from under the vocation to religious life as the Church understands and regulates it. An antihierarchical ecclesiology provides absolutely no justification for professing public vows, in particular for making a vow of obedience. At most, religious could promise *each other* that they will seek God's will, cooperate in carrying out the institute's mission, and take responsibility for participating in community affairs.[53] They have no reason to promise

---

53 This view corresponds rather well to some reinterpretations of obedience that have been proposed.

obedience to *God* unless they believe that the person who exercises authority does so in his name.[54] Those who accept the authority of the hierarchy have reason to do this because they understand that the authority the religious superior exercises "proceeds from the Spirit of the Lord" through the hierarchy, that is, because the bishop or the Holy See "has granted canonical erection to the institute and authentically approved its specific mission."[55] They accept the authority of the hierarchy—its teaching authority and jurisdiction—because they believe that Jesus Christ entrusted his ministry to them. This is an element in their faith in the Church as the unique mediator of salvation. This is what justifies the decision of religious to imitate the saving obedience of Jesus by surrendering their wills to another, whom they confidently believe mediates God's will to them.

With respect to adaptation for the needs of apostolic ministry, one might expect proponents of the "discipleship of equals" to advocate common life as a way of modeling the transformation of the Church they hope to bring about. In practice, however, it seems that the community they envision is based more on a doctrine of equal rights than on a response of self-emptying love. There is no need for a superior with personal authority in this model; it is sufficient to have a facilitator who will ensure that everyone has the opportunity to participate and that nothing is imposed that is not supported by the consensus of the group. Dialoguing with the goal of reaching such a consensus is more likely to lead to independent living, communities chosen on the basis of compatibility, or simply "hotel living" than to the witness of common life envisioned by the founders. Apart from the desire to follow Christ even to the Cross, community members with diverse "mindsets" and even diverse "belief

54 See canon 601: "The evangelical counsel of obedience, undertaken in a spirit of faith and love in the following of Christ, who was obedient even unto death, obliges submission of one's will to lawful Superiors, who act in the place of God when they give commands that are in accordance with each institute's own constitutions." Public vows, of course, must be received by a legitimate superior in the name of the Church (see canon 1192 §1).

55 SCRIS and Sacred Congregation for Bishops, *Directives for the Mutual Relations between Bishops and Religious in the Church / Mutuae relationes* (1978), 13, and *Essential Elements* (1983), 42.

systems" will not be motivated to transcend their own interests in self-emptying love.[56]

The contemporary social justice agenda has led some religious to assume the "prophetic" vocation to eradicate alleged injustices in the Church. They justify this by appealing to moments in Church history when apostolic religious brought about the doctrinal and moral reform of the hierarchy.[57] They are on a collision course with the magisterium, however, if they regard the ministerial office instituted by Christ as itself unjust or if they caution others against collaborating in the pastoral care of the faithful lest they shore up the "unjust" clerical system, or if they offer theological and pastoral alternatives to Catholics who dissent on matters of faith, morals, or discipline. Can advocates of Church reform who defy or ignore the magisterium be trusted to exercise an authentic prophetic ministry? Should those who invite apostolic religious to "leave the Church" in order to serve God's cause more faithfully be given a platform in assemblies and institutions sponsored by religious orders?[58] Why should people today be surprised when women and men religious who hold these views express no interest in the "new evangelization"?

Some Questions

Apostolic religious did not expect to become caught up in this kind of controversy, but it became unavoidable. Ideas have consequences, and the antihierarchical option continues to be tolerated and seems to enjoy the approval and support of some women and

56 For an example, see http://www.lcwr.org/lcwrprogramsresources/SystemsThinking/Handbook.pdf, 15–19. Accessed 2/10/2007. The author of the recommended manual, *An Invitation to Systems Thinking*, frankly acknowledges that community members have different "mindsets" and diverse "belief systems." In analyzing the case regarding sisters who object to "priest-led" liturgies, the author makes no appeal to the norms supplied by Catholic doctrine, much less to those that govern religious life. See *An Invitation to Systems Thinking*, 16.

57 As history shows, founders and religious orders have often called the clergy and the hierarchy to genuine reform by demonstrating an evangelical alternative, but some of these modern prophets seem to propose a politically inspired alternative.

58 Fr. Diarmuid O'Murchu, M.S.C., is being sponsored in several such institutions. For a critique of his views on religious life, see "A Doctrinal Note on the Book *Reframing Religious Life*," on http://www.ewtn.com.

men religious who serve in congregational leadership and who exercise influence in two national conferences, LCWR and CMSM. Do not these leaders unwittingly perpetuate the divisions within their institutes? Are member institutes or individuals within them free to question the directions they have taken?[59] Is a not-so-subtle attitude of resentment against the "institutional Church" being perpetuated and passed on to new generations by the very bodies that are charged with coordinating relationships with the Holy See? Are religious institutes well served? Is the Holy See well served? Is it time, perhaps, for a formal visitation?

Perhaps the crisis of "followership" is just as problematic as the crisis of leadership. How can those religious institutes that once flourished and now flounder proceed with the necessary renewal if there exist among their numbers men and women religious who have freely adopted a different ecclesiology based on the feminist critique, some other antihierarchical ideology, or the "new cosmology"? How can a superior deal with what are really irreconcilable differences among community members, not only in their ecclesiologies but in their commitment to the Catholic faith as a whole? Once the issues have been framed in terms of power and rights, leaders may feel helpless, for in the absence of a voluntary self-surrender—the free gift of self each religious makes at the time of profession—what recourse do they have? On the other hand, what responsibility do they have to their institute as a whole and to its future?

What about the hierarchy? Have our bishops turned these issues over to vicars for religious who themselves favor the "prophetic" witness aimed at reforming the hierarchy? Bishops may fear that confronting leaders of women and men religious will only make things worse. But can it actually get worse? Have they no interest in the spiritual well-being of religious who find themselves exiles in their own institutes? Have our bishops washed their hands of religious and their institutes? Are they content to extend the annual collection for the support of retired religious and move on to other

---

59 One problem, of course, is that those who have vowed obedience are reluctant to deviate from the judgment of their superiors.

matters? Religious do not expect or want bishops to tell them what to do, but they need to be part of the solution, especially for religious institutes of diocesan right.

The "Treasure" and a Fifth Challenge

What "treasure" do women and men living the apostolic religious life want to reclaim? What has been lost and what do they long for? What is the "treasure"? In the first place, the treasure is their covenant relationship with Jesus Christ, who has chosen them and whom they have chosen in return; no one can take this treasure from them. In the great winnowing of the past forty years, apostolic religious have found some way to live their consecration in intimate communion with him whatever distress they might experience in trying to live it out in their religious institutes or in the Church. St. Paul says that we bear this treasure—"the light of the knowledge of the glory of God in the face of Christ"—in earthen vessels "to show that the transcendent power belongs to God and not to us" (2 Cor 4:6–7).

However, religious cannot have Christ without the Church! They cannot claim to belong entirely to Christ and at the same time repudiate the covenant community which he established, which he loves, for which he sacrificed his life (Eph 5:25).[60] Pope Paul VI said as much in the apostolic letter *Evangelii Nuntiandi,* in response to certain antihierarchical strains in liberation theology. He refers with sorrow to well-intentioned but misguided Catholics who claim "to love Christ but without the Church, to listen to Christ but not the Church, to belong to Christ but outside the Church."[61] This dichotomy is absurd, he says, as anyone knows who recalls the Lord's saying, "Anyone who rejects you rejects me" (Lk 10:16).

To the dichotomy often proposed today, one might well add: religious cannot claim to love "the People of God" and at the same time distance themselves from the "institutional Church," those

---

60   Nor can they claim to love Christ but refuse to participate in the celebration of the New Covenant sealed in his blood, the sacrifice of the Eucharist.

61   *Evangelii Nuntiandi,* 16.

members consecrated and sent by Christ to teach, sanctify, and govern that people.[62] This dichotomy, too, depends on a distortion of Catholic doctrine; it seems to depend as well on the application of a norm extrinsic to the faith, a secular conception of "equal rights" that has no inkling of the desire for self-sacrifice that love alone inspires. The Church cannot be reduced to a sociological entity and then reinvented according to one's personal intuition about what best expresses equality. The Church is a gift from God in Christ, an internally differentiated priestly community. It cannot be the prophetic vocation of apostolic religious to repudiate the ministerial priesthood and the hierarchical structure of the Church! This does not mean there is no place for fraternal correction, for indeed it may be necessary to call one another to a more faithful living out of the Gospel. Religious may lament the failures of their brothers in the hierarchy, who like them are "earthen vessels," but they cannot reject the Church as a hierarchically structured community that mediates Christ's salvation. Religious must expect the Church's pastors, in turn, to call them to fulfill their vocation—their public, ecclesial vocation, in fact, the "prophetic" vocation entrusted to us by our founders.

The Fifth Challenge: Spiritual Renewal according to the Founding Charism

There was one more challenge the Council put to apostolic religious, namely, the challenge to spiritual renewal according to the Gospel, the legacy or charism of the founder(s), and the authentic traditions of each institute. Religious engaged this challenge years ago, but perhaps the only way to reclaim the treasure now is to return to that task with fresh vigor and determination. If apostolic religious want to regain the moral authority they once enjoyed, if they long for that "full participation" in the Church's life which is identical with holiness, the perfection of charity, they must "start

---

62   See Avery Cardinal Dulles, "Nature, Mission, and Structure of the Church," in *Vatican II: Renewal within Tradition,* ed. Matthew L. Lamb and Matthew Levering, 3–36 (Oxford: Oxford University Press, 2008).

afresh from Christ"[63] and from the charism of our founders, free of "politically correct" considerations. Why did their founders request canonical status? What is the ideal that attracted them to their institutes? How faithfully are they expressing it? What can these institutes offer the Church today?

It is necessary to study, along with our founding stories and documents, the many exhortations addressed to apostolic religious by the Holy See—from *Perfectae Caritatis* to the most recent instruction on Authority and Obedience. These must be studied and used for individual and communal self-examination. Are religious still willing to serve? Do they still desire to profess the poverty, chastity, and obedience of Jesus Christ "freely, willingly, and purely for the love of God"? Can they help each other to do this?

The "treasure" many religious wish to reclaim, perhaps, is the possibility of living the religious life fully, in peace, according to the charism of their communities, in communion with the hierarchy and collaboration with the laity, that is, according to the ecclesiology of communion, "one in heart and soul" (Acts 4:32) with others in the Church. Beyond that, the "treasure" might be the confidence that their consecration makes a difference; that they belong to Christ and to his Church in and through the mediation of their religious institutes, and that their charism and mission are valued by others in the Church—laity and hierarchy—as a gift of the Holy Spirit. Religious want to get beyond the stress of being suspicious and being under suspicion, and enter into a realm where they are recognized as a resource, where they are needed and wanted, where they can make a corporate impact through ministerial service that is coordinated with or supplements the plans of dioceses and the initiatives of the universal Church.[64]

---

63 The CICLSAL issued this powerful invitation to persons in the consecrated life at the outset of the 21st century in "Starting Afresh from Christ: A Renewed Commitment to Consecrated Life in the Third Millennium" (*Origins* 32 [July 4, 2002]: 129, 131–48).

64 Where these supportive relationships are in place, we are free to be creative, and we can flourish through the ups and downs that inevitably attend ministry. This requires mutual trust, a trust that can be rebuilt only if our members can be counted on to support the Church's teaching and discipline and to collaborate generously with diocesan clergy and laity under the direction of the bishop.

Those who choose to remain, and who embrace the obligation to live the religious life as the Holy See defines it, long for the rebirth of relationships in which their place in the Church is clear and unambiguous, and in which they can ask of one another the witness of holiness according to the nature, purpose, and spirit of their institutes. Religious must strive to develop apostolic initiatives that will allow them to live and work together so that their efforts will build up the Church, give striking witness to her mission, and attract vocations so that their charism will continue to be a gift to the Church. May we who are apostolic religious keep our eyes on the "treasure." May we renew our willingness to "sell everything" to possess it.

Three

"*De Accommodata Renovatione:* Between the Idea and the Reality..."

Occasion and Intent and Consequences of Vatican Council II

ELIZABETH MCDONOUGH, O.P.

These reflections arise from my being one among thousands of "BC" sisters. "BC" refers to those who entered religious life before or during Vatican Council II and obviously had not a clue about what was on the not-too-distant horizon.[1] In January 1959, when

---

1 These are "20/20" observations regarding the slightly more than four decades since Vatican Council II concluded. They are chronologically "20/20" because major transitions in religious life can be identified from the conclusion of that Council in 1965 to the work of the Quinn Commission in the mid-1980s (see n. 7 below), and from that Commission's final report to the present. These observations are also "20/20" because hindsight is a perspective from which past events are usually much clearer than when they occurred. These observations are distilled from nearly a decade in religious life before implementation of Vatican II began and from slightly more than three decades thereafter. Apostolic endeavors, professional contributions, and experience during these three decades include: canonical consultation for more than two hundred religious communities (women and men) in the United States and abroad; consultation for more than a dozen

John XXIII announced the Second Vatican Council (along with revision of the 1917 Code of Canon Law), my religious community had more than seven hundred sisters, operated two colleges and three high school academies, staffed more than three dozen grade schools and high schools in six states, and owned and operated a small hospital. Having twenty or more novices a year was a common occurrence. Office was chanted in Latin daily. Permission was required to write home (back then you never phoned home). Full habit was worn whether teaching or waxing floors or playing basketball, and "chapter of faults" was held monthly.

In 1984, a quarter century after the Council was announced, our prioress sent me to Rome to apologize personally on her behalf to Cardinal Hamer, prefect of the Congregation for Religious and Secular Institutes, because—without her knowledge or permission—one of our sisters had signed the full-page ad published in the *New York Times* on Pro-Life Sunday (October 7th), thus publicly affirming agreement with others who espoused "a diversity of opinion" among "committed Catholics" regarding abortion. Our prioress wanted the Holy See to know this action did not represent who we were or what we were about as Dominican women religious in the Church. We were not—she said—in the business of embarrassing the hierarchy and were certainly not among those espousing positions contrary to Church teaching. Recently, this same (former) prioress remarked that a quarter century ago sisters here or there might take stands contrary to Church teaching, but now it is those in leadership who do so, often frequently and often very publicly and often applauding other religious who do the same.

About a quarter century after 1984, the religious congregation to which I belonged had one-third as many sisters, operated two

arch/dioceses; and consultation on more than forty misconduct cases (one-tenth of which involved religious). They also include: teaching canon law and/or theology at the graduate level to priests, deacons, and seminarians for seventeen years; serving as delegate of the Apostolic See in 1991 for final stages of the merger of the Institute of the Sisters of Mercy of the Americas (see n. 2 below); assisting in the recent Apostolic Visitation of Seminaries; authoring one book, several book chapters, and more than thirty articles in canonical journals; and (since summer 1990) contributing one hundred successive "Canonical Counsel" essays in *Review for Religious* as its canonical editor.

colleges and one academy, and staffed half a dozen schools in three states. In 2008 there were three new professions, and we were one of only fifty-six congregations adequately funded for retirement according to National Religious Retirement Office (NRRO) standards. In early 2009, this religious congregation ceased to exist as it joined six other Dominican congregations in a canonical union.[2] This tripled the number of senior sisters, significantly raised the median age, and resulted in less than adequate retirement funding for all sisters involved since the adequate retirement funding for one congregation simply could not provide adequate NRRO retirement funds for all seven combined. It seems fair to say that the religious community to which I belonged was certainly not alone in the changes it underwent during the last three decades, including recent "reconfiguration" by merging into one, larger religious institute.

It also seems fair to ask how it happened that so many communities of women religious in the United States may have arrived at the brink of becoming an ecclesiastical version of "ENRON" writ large on the not-so-distant-horizon after nearly a half-century in which thousands upon thousands of sisters tried diligently and, for the most part, quite honestly to implement as best they could the sweeping challenges Vatican Council II asked of them.

2   A canonical union is often referred to as a merger and is now commonly called a "reconfiguration." A major merger (union) of multiple communities of Sisters of Mercy in the United States occurred in 1991. The Mercy merger was more than fifteen years in preparation and became a blueprint for current reconfigurations. In 1991, there were more than eight thousand Sisters of Mercy in the United States. Today there are fewer than four thousand. For a detailed explanation of this union, see the doctoral dissertation of Catherine C. Darcy, R.S.M., *The Institute of the Sisters of Mercy of the Americas: The Canonical Development of the Proposed Governance Model* (Lanham, Md.: University Press of America, 1993).

On April 12, 2009, my religious institute of initial profession ceased to exist in the same kind of canonical union as it and six other congregations were simultaneously, formally suppressed by the Apostolic See (canon 584). Prior to this, twenty-two sisters of my original congregation (including this author) received indults of departure (canon 691), which took effect upon profession of perpetual vows in the Dominican Sisters of Our Lady of the Springs of Bridgeport, a new diocesan religious institute formally established on April 2, 2009, by the Most Rev. William E. Lori, bishop of Bridgeport, with prior ecclesiastical approval from the Congregation for Institutes of Consecrated Life and Societies of Apostolic Life. All twenty-two sisters made a new perpetual profession April 3–11, 2009.

From the advantage of hindsight, it seems evident that—whatever anyone may think, say, hope, or regret about Vatican II—hardly anyone senses that the intent of the Council and its genuine potential have been realized. Certainly its call for *accommodata renovatio* of religious life has yet to be realized. Indeed, it is possible that renewal for religious as mandated by the Council may not yet even have begun. In hindsight, it appears that the greatest contribution of Vatican Council II may have been the hope that its bold and broad-ranging challenges would engender in the entire Church a deeply profound and interior conversion, as well as a comprehensive intellectual and volitional conversion, at all levels of ecclesial life. If this could be accomplished, then this truly Catholic Church might offer ever more effectively to this increasingly complex and troubled world the salvation truly wrought by Jesus Christ alone. If this was the hope of the Council, that hope is still alive.

Reflecting on the Council's consequences, however, there seem to have been several mistakes—some small and others (perhaps) not so small—in the understanding and implementation of the Council's call for renewal; these have gradually resulted in significant errors and/or obvious negative consequences for religious life in the United States.

These small or not-so-small mistakes relate to: (1) the Council's *context;* (2) the *challenges* of *Perfectae Caritatis* compared to the *competence* (or lack) of those implementing it; (3) the genuine *theological confusion* arising from functional conciliar decisions; and (4) forty years of *confrontation* and *compromise* in oversight by the hierarchy.

Context of the Council

The historical context setting the stage for multiple unforeseen consequences of the Council was the tumultuous decade of the 1960s. By human standards it would seem to have been exactly the wrong time for the Council to have occurred. From beginning to end the 1960s was a period of ongoing global, cultural, social, and political upheavals. To mention a few in the United States: that decade took us rapidly (shockingly, at times) from the assassination of John F. Kennedy to the student deaths at Kent State University, from the Cuban missile crisis to the Tet offensive in Vietnam, from the Los Angeles riots to the riots at the Democratic National Convention in Chicago, from Martin Luther King's "I Have a Dream" speech to his assassination, and from *The Sound of Music* at the decade's beginning to the decidedly different sounds of Woodstock at its end.

The decade of the 1960s also saw a revival of earlier feminist movements in society and in the Church.[3] Social feminism readily critiqued oppression and dysfunction in gender relations, while liberal feminism began to call for total egalitarian gender rights. The next decade saw liberal feminism in the civil sector evolve into radical feminism, which condemned patriarchy as the cause of all social domination. By the late 1960s, Mary Daly's *The Church and the Second Sex* (1968) had called the question on sexism in the Church. Beginning in the 1970s, and echoing Daly, radical-liberal feminism in the Church condemned patriarchy and hierarchy as causes of all ecclesial domination.[4]

---

3   Sara Butler, M.S.B.T., "Women and the Church" in *Gift of the Church,* ed. Peter C. Phan (Collegeville, Minn.: Liturgical Press, 2000): 415–33. The same basic divisions of feminist movements in society are described by Sandra Schneiders, I.H.M., *Beyond Patching: Faith and Feminism in the Catholic Church* (Mahwah, N.J.: Paulist Press, 1991) 15–25. Schneiders (16) makes clear that "feminism is a comprehensive theoretical system for analyzing, criticizing, and evaluating ideas, social structures, procedures and practices, indeed the whole of experienced reality. But it is more than a theoretical system for criticism because it involves the proposal of an alternative vision and a commitment to bring that vision to socio-political realization."

4   Schneiders, *Beyond Patching,* summarizes the approach of radical-liberal feminism and its position regarding the Catholic Church in some detail. On framing the issue, see 4: "The seamless garment of the body of Christ, an ancient image of the unity of the church, has grown old and thin and faded. The sins of patriarchy, notable sexism, clericalism, and racism, have created great tears in the fabric of unity. Some in the church would like to see feminism as a patch that can be sewn, inconspicuously they hope, over the rips and tears of division. But those who would reduce feminism to a local repair job on an otherwise still useable garment risk aggravating rather than improving the situation. Feminism is not a patch; it is a whole new pattern which can only be realized by weaving a new garment." See 18–26, for "The Critique of Patriarchy" in general, and 31–36 for "Feminism in the Church." The objective is clear at 36: "Women do not seek to participate as imitation males or on male terms in a male construction of reality. Rather they have undertaken a deconstruction of male reality and a reconstruction of reality in more human terms." The means of accomplishing this are listed at 105–6: "Catholic feminists . . . are not content to

Liberal-feminist influences quickly co-opted—that is, preempted and began to control—the (then) Conference of Major Religious Superiors of Women's Institutes, changing it into the Leadership Conference of Women Religious by 1971.[5] Vatican officials noticed the difference but failed to recognize or to address LCWR's political agenda as well as the underlying ideology and methodology of its radical transformation.[6] During the mid-1980s LCWR (with the apparent cooperation of the Conference of Major Superiors of Men) successfully co-opted Pope John Paul II's attempt to assess the state of religious life in the United States by means of a "pastoral service" to be implemented by the bishops at the time of the Quinn Commission.[7]

---

await, actively or passively, the reform of the institutional church. They have undertaken to develop rituals which not only do not oppress them but will give them life and hope. They do not hesitate to rewrite the stories of tradition from the standpoint of women's experience, to repudiate the stories from the tradition which marginalize, demonize, or degrade them, and to write new stories which carry the non-patriarchal content of the tradition in ways that are meaningful for women. . . . Many have taken anti-establishment positions on such issues as contraception, divorce and remarriage, homosexuality, and abortion."

5 For various interpretations of this transition, see: George A. Kelly, *The Battle for the American Church* (Garden City, N.Y.: Image Books, 1981) 289–294; Lora Ann Quiñonez, C.D.P., and Mary Daniel Turner, S.N.D.deN., "From CMSW to LCWR: A Story of Birth and Transformation," *Review for Religious* 49 (1990): 295–302; and Ann Carey, *Sisters in Crisis* (Huntington, Ind.: Our Sunday Visitor Press, 1997) 84–107. A later, more detailed treatment of this transition can be found in Quiñonez and Turner, *The Transformation of American Catholic Sisters* (Philadelphia: Temple University Press, 1992). See especially, ch. 1, "Changing Times," at 18, for the organizational restructuring of 1968–1971"; 28, for the "process of reidentification;" 30, and for "the refashioning of religious life."

6 See Quiñonez and Turner, *The Transformation of American Catholic Sisters*, especially ch. 4, "Their Name is 'Woman,'" 88–112, for the pervasive influence of feminism on the original Conference of Major Religious Superiors of Women as it was transformed into the Leadership Conference of Women Religious. See also, the index, under "Feminization of Sisters." Turner was executive director of LCWR 1972–1978, and Quiñonez was executive director of LCWR 1978–1986.

7 On Easter Sunday 1983, Pope John Paul II wrote the bishops of the United States asking them to study reasons for the decline in apostolic religious and to ascertain possible means to be of service to them. Archbishop John Quinn of San Francisco was appointed head of a commission (commonly known as the "Quinn Commission") to oversee this study. The letter to the bishops described their task as "a pastoral service," and it was accompanied by an unsigned document of guidelines prepared by the Congregation for Religious. The guidelines relied on the new 1983 Code of Canon Law as well as on various conciliar and post-conciliar documents, papal exhortations, etc. Commonly known as "Essential Elements," the guidelines were intended to assist bishops in evaluating renewal.

Meanwhile, leadership of multiple LCWR communities had begun redefining the charism of their institutes as a global social justice–oriented "mission" requiring internal structural change and
then initiated "reconfiguration" of multiple communities into large
global feminist-operated business corporations. Power (not authority) became concentrated in top-level administrators who could
deliver a "corporate impact" by determining the "mission" while
controlling all structures and resources in what was (formerly identifiable as) a religious institute.[8] Movable assets began to be con-
sumed in new endeavors, as congregations discovered they had only
minimal control over institutions they had founded and operated for
many decades. Leadership, now in complete control of a redefined
form of religious life considered merely as a series of evolving moments, could also regularly redefine the "mission" and "quietly retire"
older versions of the mission as needed.[9] By the mid 1990s, those

---

But the document soon became a flashpoint of controversy and even a litmus test for as-
sessing various aspects of what had occurred in religious life since Vatican II. The Quinn
Commission Report of October 1986 noted the impact on religious life of cultural factors
and various other Vatican II documents, as well as multiple sociological transitions, the
blurring of corporate identity, and the influence of personal choices. But the report also
stated that "our three years' work leads us to believe that in general religious life in the
United States is in good condition." *Origins* (December 4, 1986): 467–70. See Ann Carey,
"The Quinn Commission Examines Religious Life," 211–233, which summarizes several
controversial matters regarding religious women in the United States that occurred during the Quinn Commission study, including Mercy Sister Agnes Mary Mansour's acceptance of a political appointment in the State of Michigan and the October 1984 *New York
Times* ad affirming an alternative opinion on the Church's position regarding abortion.
See Quinonez and Turner, *The Transformation of American Catholic Sisters*, 86–87, 138–39.
    8   Jean Alvarez, "Focusing a Congregation's Future," *Human Development* 5 (Winter
1984): 25–34. Alvarez admitted that her "focus" replaced Aristotle's final, efficient, formal,
and material causes (respectively) with mission, power, structure, and resources to pro-
duce a corporate reorganization within religious institutes such that all decision making
would be restricted to direct or indirect control by top-level administrators. See Elizabeth
McDonough, O.P., "Juridical Deconstruction of Religious Institutes," *Studia Canonica* 26
(1992): 307–41, especially 322n16.
    9   Alvarez, "Focusing a Congregation's Future," 31. The influence on communities
of women religious of corporate reorganization through mission can hardly be underestimated. See also, Mary Trainor, R.S.M., "A Participative Approach to Corporate Restructuring in the World of Religious Women," a paper presented to the Conference on Coalitions
at Boston University, May 1988, introduction. Frequently cited in the Darcy dissertation
(n. 2, above), Trainor favored the movement to unite the multiple Mercy congregations in
the United States. She analyzes the origins, operative principles, and strategies of this Mercy corporate reorganization and summarizes them thus: "The dynamic transformation of

fostering and implementing the corporate-oriented reorganization of religious institutes effectively convinced ordinary sisters and the Roman Curia that adopting it was in accord with the provisions of *Perfectae Caritatis* 22. The truth is that formation of these global social justice–oriented feminist business corporations has nothing to do with the renewal challenges of Vatican II at all. Recently, to its credit, the Congregation for Institutes of Consecrated Life and Societies of Apostolic Life has begun to recognize this.

Challenges of *Perfectae Caritatis* and Competence for Implementation

Perfectae Caritatis (hereafter, *PC*) was obviously comprehensive in its call for renewal, so problems with its consequent implementation should not have been surprising. Religious were asked to make their way of life new again *(re-novatio)* by suitable, appropriate measures through continuous return to the sources of Christian life and to the original inspiration of their institutes. Under the impulse of the Holy Spirit and the guidance of the Church, they were to adjust their entire life to the changed conditions of the times with the added, timely caution that even the best possible adjustments would be ineffective if not fundamentally animated by a spiritual renewal

relationship and governance currently underway among twenty-six groups of Sisters of Mercy . . . evolved out of a shared vision of how [they] could more effectively accomplish their common mission. . . . It is a story of voluntary corporate restructuring, a social change envisioned and initiated by leadership, and worked out in collaboration with the membership." In retrospect, Trainor draws a parallel between the corporate restructuring then occurring and the 1929 canonical union of twenty-nine Mercy congregations into the Sisters of Mercy of the Union, stating that "a change in the interpretation of the charism by persuasive leadership persons mediated the change in governance structures" at that time (see 17). She then compares the 1929 canonical union to the current merger process, which (she explains) was initiated after a 1981 sesquicentennial celebration attended by more than one thousand Mercy sisters. Shortly thereafter, the Governing Board of the Federation of R.S.M.s in the United States envisioned a common charism of "corporate mission" among Mercies at national and global levels. Trainor also points out (see 28–29) that "this concept of corporate mission represents a paradigm shift (i.e., a radical change in the framework which defines our understanding of mission)." For the very different circumstances that prompted initiation of the 1929 canonical union of Mercy sisters, see Justine Sabourin, R.S.M., *The Amalgamation: A History of the Union of the Religious Sisters of Mercy in the United States of America* (St. Meinrad, Ind.: Abbey Press, 1976), 6–9.

(*PC* 2). The living, praying, working, and governing aspects of religious life were to be harmonized in keeping with the nature of the institute, apostolic needs, cultural demands, social and economic circumstances, and the like. Thus, all constitutions, directories, custom books, prayer books, and so on were to be duly adjusted in keeping with Council documents such that anything obsolete in them was to be suppressed (*PC* 3).[10] All members were to be involved in this *re-novatio,* although introducing experiments explicitly belonged only to competent authorities, and faithful observance was clearly affirmed as more important than multiplying norms (*PC* 4).

One very significant negative consequence of the ongoing process of renewal resulted from apparent lack of foresight on the part of the (then) Sacred Congregation for Religious regarding the extent, duration, difficulty, and complexity of implementing *PC*'s multiple challenges. That dicastery seems to have greatly underestimated the timeline for finalizing revisions as well as the degree of alteration that resulted from the mandated renewal chapters. Subsequently, personnel of that dicastery simply could not keep pace with the volume of texts arriving in Rome in rapid-fire fashion that needed careful review and eventual approval. Even more so, multiple *contra legem* experiments flourished and gradually became the rule rather than the exception.[11] As time passed and versions of constitution revisions multiplied, the Congregation for Religious formally approved documents apparently unaware of possible variant meanings in generic wording that could be used to provide for interpretations, applications, or alterations quite different from those ordinarily expected or employed by curial officials.[12]

---

10   In retrospect, it is fair to ask if those who mandated revision of all community documents as worded in this cryptic, significant text may have had any idea of its possible far-reaching, long-term consequences: "Quapropter constitutiones, 'directoria,' libri usuum, precum et caeremoniarum aliique id genus codices, congruenter recognoscantur atque, iis prascriptis suppressis quae obsoleta sint, documentis huius Sacrae Synodi aptentur."

11   Joseph M. Becker, S.J., *The Re-Formed Jesuits,* vol.1: *A History of Changes in Jesuit Formation during the Decade 1965–1975* (San Francisco: Ignatius Press, 1992), documents how gradual alteration of previously mandated practices eventually became the norm. Sisters can readily trace such changes in their own congregational documents.

12   A common example (with evident, widespread consequences) would be inclu-

A second very significant negative consequence of this ongoing process was that the Curia both overestimated and underestimated resources for renewal among women religious. Overestimation concerned the philosophical, theological, spiritual, and canonical background of women religious, most of whom had only minimal or no knowledge of these fields in the 1960s. At first, communities of women religious relied extensively on various religious clergy for this assistance. But some of these advisors presented very different approaches for renewal than *PC* had articulated; sisters who were encouraged to go beyond or to ignore various aspects of *PC* seemed to do so willingly, often because a diocesan or religious priest had recommended it.[13]

In turn, the Curia either did not recognize or vastly underestimated the feminist-oriented social-justice agenda of women religious in the Unites States that had begun to emerge as early as 1964.[14] This agenda quickly became prominent in the transition from CMSW to LCWR by 1970. When the "Transformative Elements of Religious Life" were jointly affirmed by LCWR and CMSM in 1989, this agenda became public and—for the most part—has been totally unchecked.[15] Recently, however, more faithful laity, women religious, and mem-

sion of the statement in *PC 17* on habit in newly revised constitutions using very generic wording, such as: "Our religious attire is a sign of consecration and a witness to poverty. It is simple and modest and appropriate to our lifestyle and apostolate. It is described in the Directory." But after initial approval of both the Constitutions and Directory by higher ecclesiastical authority (as required), a later general chapter could alter or even delete the description in the Directory with no further approval required. Thus, it was possible that, within a short time, no specific requirement for any identifiable religious attire (habit) would appear anywhere in either the approved Constitutions or Directory.

13 David Fleming, S.M., "Community, Corporateness, and Communion," in *Starting Points,* ed. Lora Ann Quiñonez, C.D.P., 33–44 (Washington, D.C.: LCWR, 1980); Thomas E. Clarke, S.J., "Whose Life Is It?," in ibid., 87–116; *Renewal through Community and Experimentation* (Washington, D.C.: Canon Law Society of America, 1968). Also see Carey, *Sisters in Crisis,* 82.

14 Sister M. Charles Borromeo Muckenhirn, C.S.C., ed., *The Changing Sister* (Notre Dame, Ind.: Fides, 1965), details its beginning before conclusion of the Council. Idem., *The Implications of Renewal* (Notre Dame, Ind.: Fides, 1967) devotes 130 pages to renewal of religious life, culminating with her version of "The Nun of the Future" (274–94).

15 Marie Augusta Neal, S.N.D.deN., *Catholic Sisters in Transition* (Wilmington, Del.: Michael Glazier, 1984), and *From Nuns to Sisters* (Mystic, Conn.: Twenty-Third Publications, 1990). Note that, in parallel contrast to the "Essential Elements" of 1983, the CMSM/LCWR Joint Assembly of 1989 issued ten "Transformative Elements" for moving

bers of the hierarchy are now recognizing that the long-term feminist agenda has been more than slightly harmful to consecrated life in the Church.

Functional Council Decisions with Significant Theological Consequences

Religious life is supposed to bring "following Christ more closely" (*sequela Christi pressius*) to the level of lifestyle according to a par-

---

religious life into the future, specifically citing a target date of 2010. These appeared shortly after Pope John Paul II's comments on the "Quinn Commission Report" were sent to bishops who participated in a March 1989 meeting about its results. (See nn. 7 and 31–32). With the benefit of two decades of hindsight, at least some of these ten "Transformative Elements" (i.e., 1, 5, 6, 8, 9, quoted here) do seem to have influenced major changes in religious life since 1989:

1 *Prophetic Witness*—Being converted by the example of Jesus and the values of the gospel, religious in the year 2010 will serve a prophetic role in church and society. Living this prophetic witness will include critiquing societal and ecclesial values and structures, calling for systemic change and being converted by the marginalized with whom we serve.

5 *Charism and Mission as Sources of Identity*—By the year 2010, religious groups will have reexamined, reclaimed and set free the charisms of their foundresses/founders. Corporate ownership of a focused vision gives meaning and expression to mission and ministry. Some groups who share similar visions/charisms have already joined together.

6 *Change of the Locus of Power*—Religious in 2010 will have replaced models of domination with principles of mutuality drawn from feminist and theological insights, so that collaborative modes of decision making and power sharing are normative. Priorities for service will be generated and shaped in the local arena while impetus for such action will be influenced by global awareness.

8 *Broad-based, Inclusive Community*—In 2010 religious communities will be characterized by inclusivity and intentionality. These communities may include persons of different ages, genders, cultures, races, and sexual orientation. They may include persons who are lay or cleric, married or single, or as vowed and/or unvowed members. They will have a core group and persons with temporary and permanent commitments. These communities will be ecumenical, possibly interfaith; faith sharing will be constitutive of the quality of life in this context of expanded membership. Such inclusivity will necessitate a new understanding of membership and a language to accompany it. Religious life still includes religious congregations of permanently vowed members.

9 *Understanding Ourselves as Church*—An essential element of religious life in 2010 is our ability to accept the concept that "we are church." As people of God, we assume our priestly role of shared leadership in the life and worship of the local church. We support all members of the church as equals in diverse ministries.

ticular charism through consecration by vow. This consecration is recognized by the Church as placing anyone who becomes "a religious" in a different category than does ordination or marriage or remaining single. Moreover, perpetually vowed religious life is a category of consecration recognized as a fundamental part of the Church's complete structure, though not part of its hierarchical structure. While *PC* included specific mention of other forms of consecrated life such as secular institutes, its title and content were primarily directed to *renovatio vitae religiosae*, the clearly predominant category at that time. As it happens, a change in the final format of *Lumen Gentium* (hereafter *LG*) before its approval in late 1964 had immense consequences for altering the theological interpretation of religious vows as they later appeared in *Perfectae Caritatis* in the fall of 1965. The traditional order of the vows (poverty-chastity-obedience) was changed in *PC* solely because of the changed order in which they had already appeared in *LG*. After the Council, some theologians quickly interpreted this change in the order of the vows as intentional and also theologically significant. Subsequently, the change in order and these instant, unsubstantiated interpretations created great confusion about the import of professing these evangelical counsels by vow in religious life.

Even without detailed explanation of the transitions and multiple revisions of what eventually became the *Dogmatic Constitution on the Church* (*Lumen Gentium*), it is obvious that chapter 5, "The Universal Call to Holiness" (nn39–42), and chapter 6, "On Religious" (nn43–47), are both very brief. This is because chapters 5 and 6 had been in a single chapter (chapter 5 on the "Call to Holiness") until it was split into its present form in September 1964. This split occurred at the insistence of bishops who were themselves religious and of superiors general of men's religious communities who participated fully in the Council. The *Acta Synodalia* explanation for where the split in chapter 5 occurred states that the point at which vows were first mentioned was considered an appropriate transition from one expression of holiness to another. It was, according to official documentation in the *Acta Synodalia*, simply a convenient point requiring little change in wording, which provided a "quamdam transitionem ab uno ad aliud argumentum" and thus a simple "transitus fit ad Religiosos." Comments of the Doctrinal Commission for interpretation of the separation explicitly note that this division into two chapters did not contradict or reject or change any prior documents of the Church's magisterium.[16] Chapter 6 of *LG* begins with chastity because the previous sentences (still in chapter 5) had first treated charity as full perfection of the law in Christian discipleship and then noted martyrdom as the supreme imitation of Christ. It then highlighted the preeminence and high honor of virginity or celibacy among the multiple counsels proposed by the Lord and emphasized the charity and humility of those who follow Christ in poverty and obedience. Chapter 5 of *LG* then concluded by summarizing and reaffirming the call given to all to seek the one holiness offered by, and perfectly manifest in, Jesus Christ.

Thus, chapter 6, "De Religiosis," begins by mentioning the three counsels in the order they appeared when it was still part of the original chapter 5 of *LG*. No theological reason was given for reversing the order of poverty and chastity in the traditional triad of poverty-chastity-obedience, and it is clear that chastity was listed first in the longer, original chapter 5 because that chapter's format was to comment briefly on the many specific expressions of the universal call to holiness. But this functional split of chapter 5 at the logically optimal point for a *transitus* to the new chapter 6 soon acquired a significance and significantly problematic theological "life of its own."

Lumen Gentium was promulgated in late 1964. The amended

16 *Acta Synodalia Sacrosancti Concilii Oecumenici Vaticani II*, vol. 3, Periodus Tertia, pars III, 65 and especially 67–68: "Quoad particularia attendendum est ad ipsam exegesim obiectivam textus. Ad hoc autem faciendum iuvat etiam mentem commissionis cognoscere. Quae mens praesertim ex actibus sive subcommissionis sive commissionis innotescit. Propositum in redigendo textu fuit, ut etiam obiective constet, neque selectam fuisse unam vel aliam scholarum methodologiam, neque, ut obvium est, anterioribus documentis Magisterii Ecclesiae contradicere vel in aliquo doctrinaliter immutare, neque recipere vel profiteri nec reicere ea quae in presenti sunt liberae disceptionis inter theologos. Monuit enim nuperrime etiam Em.mus Cardinalis Decanus hoc Concilium non intendere novas proponere doctrinas. Consequenter, quamvis differentia, praesentia et momentum status religiosi in Ecclesia clarius appareat ex capite distincto religiosis dedecato, tamen ex votatione Concilii circa hoc, qualemcumque exitum heabeat, doctrinaliter nihil novum deduci potest aut debet."

text of *Perfectae Caritatis,* which appeared in fall 1965, listed the vows (nn12, 13, 14) in the order of chastity-poverty-obedience. No prior schema of *PC* had done so. The change in order of the vows in the 1965 text of *PC* occurred only because *Lumen Gentium* had already been promulgated. That is, 441 of the Council Fathers had explicitly requested that the order of the vows in *PC* be chastity-poverty-obedience so that it would correspond to the order of the vows as they had already appeared in *LG* chapter 6.[17] Very many other interventions had requested retaining the traditional order of the vows as poverty-chastity-obedience because of the significance of progressive renunciation of legitimate "goods" in the theological explanation of that vow sequence. As it happened, the higher number of 441 who favored the sequence as already promulgated in *LG* prevailed.[18]

Before the explanation of the Doctrinal Commission was published in the *Acta Synodalia,* some authors began to speculate—without access to primary sources—that a clear theological change had occurred in the understanding of religious vows precisely because of the new order in which they now appeared. Jesuits Paul Molinari and Peter Gumpbel claimed it was "not difficult *to guess* the reasons which led the Doctrinal Commission to abandon the traditional order and place virginity first"[19] [emphasis added]. They then asserted that listing virginity first clearly showed the Council Fathers' emphasis on the importance of charity in undivided love as primarily indicative of religious life. After briefly outlining the theology for the classical order of the vows, they stated that this for-

17 *Acta Synodalia,* vol. 4, pars IV, 535: "Quoad ordinem conciliorum plures modi propununtur: (a) Circa 450 Patres postulant ordinem sequentem 'castitas—paupertas—oboedientia' (cf. p. 11, n. 3). *Ratio: ut hic ordo respondeat ordini consiliorum in Constitutione dogmatica 'De Ecclesia'* (b) Alii volunt retinere ordinem: 'paupertas—castitas—oboedientia' (cf. pp. 11–12, n. 4). *Ratio: hic ordo est traditionalis et ostendit progressionem quamdam 'vi cuius religious renunciat bonis quae habet'"*[emphasis added].

18 *Acta Synodalia,* vol. 4, pars III. Votes and comments are at 529, 531, 535 and 560. At 560, the number requesting a change in the order to correspond to *Lumen Gentium* is recorded as 441.

19 Paul Molinari, S.J., and Peter Gumpbel, S.J., *Chapter VI of the Dogmatic Constitution "Lumen Gentium" on Religious Life: The Doctrinal Content in the Light of the Official Documents* (Milan: Ancora, 1987), 84.

mer order (poverty-chastity-obedience) "failed to provide any explanation for the intrinsic connection" among them.[20] Juan Lozano, C.M.F., also rejected in very brief fashion the late, great triad of poverty-chastity-obedience and then devoted thirty pages of comments to "Celibacy for the Sake of the Kingdom."[21]

Thus, the functionally convenient point for splitting chapter 5 of *LG* into two chapters resulted in almost instant theologically influential interpretations through convincing—but unsubstantiated—speculation that had no basis in the reasons for the Council's decision. Quite ironically, the desire to avoid confusion about the order of the vows in two different Council documents resulted in rather rapid theological dismissal of the poverty-chastity-obedience triad, and this has since caused immense theological confusion about the vows as central to the consecration unique to religious life as such. This mistaken theological speculation has also had important consequences because consecration in religious life really is supposed to bring the gift to the Church of a God-given charism to the level of a specific lifestyle in following Christ more closely. My decidedly Dominican perspective regarding current confusion in the understanding of religious vows is that if those of us who are religious cannot get the basic theology of our religious life straight, then we are never going to get the basics of our lives as religious straight.

Since by functional circumstance a new sequence of vows beginning with chastity prevailed, feminist theologians could rapidly redefine the theological meaning of religious vows to support progressive practices already evident in implementation of *PC* by myriads of women religious. Sandra Schneiders, I.H.M., explained at great length how this new order of the vows made consecrated celibacy a "constitutive charism" manifesting the radicality and absoluteness of religious life, which—she asserted—has nothing necessarily to do with community or with ministry as such.[22] In the early

20 Ibid., 85–86.
21 Juan Lozano, C.M.F., *Discipleship: Towards an Understanding of Religious Life* (Chicago: Claret Center for Resources in Spirituality, 1980), 120 and 140–71.
22 Sandra Schneiders, I.H.M., *Selling All: Commitment, Consecrated Celibacy, and Community in Catholic Religious Life* (Mahwah, N.J.: Paulist Press, 2001). See chapter 4,

Church, she explained, consecrated virgins could live "singly" or in groups of their own choosing for basic companionship and could then cooperate effectively for mutual spiritual and temporal assistance. When living in such freely chosen groups, sharing of goods was appropriate as a forerunner of poverty, and communal cooperation among consecrated virgins of equal status was certainly preferable to any later, distorted development of obedience to a single superior. No matter that only women can be consecrated as virgins through an ancient liturgical ceremony even though religious life has been embraced by both men and women for nearly two millennia. No matter that origins of cenobitical monasticism did not begin merely with virginity. Though monks and nuns were required to be celibate, it was also an early requirement that no one with personal assets would be accepted into cenobitical monastic life until these assets were given away completely. Why? Because it was readily realized that fundamental elements of life together could not be sustained if those committed to a community retained personal "nest eggs" that permitted them to do whatever they wanted, whenever they wanted, independent from their commitment to, and with, the rest of the community. From the beginning, it was obvious that common life could readily be undermined or simply be abandoned by those with personal assets whenever daily circumstances of actual life in common failed to meet their personal expectations. It was just as obvious that those without personal assets simply had to stick around.

These entirely new explanations of the new order of vows conveniently rendered religious life as a purely personal, cooperative en-

---

"Celibacy as Charism," 117–200, esp. 125–32 and 145–49. Affirmation of chastity as "constitutive" of religious life with no necessary connection to ministry seems contrary to the statement in "Transformative Element" #5 that "charism and mission" will be future "Sources of Identity" and that "Corporate ownership of a focused vision gives meaning and expression to mission and ministry" (n. 15, above). Chastity as "constitutive" of religious life with no essential role for any ministry also contrasts greatly with trends toward widespread corporate reorganization of religious institutes during the last three decades (see nn. 8 and 9, above). Relegation of ministry to a nonessential side effect also seems contrary to claims of progressive apostolic religious institutes, which often present what they actually do in ministry as the primary example of—as well as the determining factor for—their identity and mission as religious.

deavor recognized by the Church but with no reference to its prior communal or obediential aspects as understood for more than 1,500 years. In this fashion, hundreds of women religious living alone in apartments could be described simply as living "singly," like consecrated virgins in the early Church. And, in Schneiders's assessment, most women religious living "singly" do so primarily for spiritual reasons[23] and are no less observant or less poor or less obedient than those living in common. This theologically unfounded justification of the post–Vatican II drift to apartment living by many women religious certainly supported already established practices of progressive religious institutes, but it left other religious and clergy and laity with a widespread sense of genuine cognitive dissonance.

Thus, the functional separation of *LG* chapter 5 into chapters 5 and 6 at the comment on virginity, which then changed the order in *PC* to chastity-poverty-obedience by majority vote in order to avoid confusion, has inadvertently resulted in immense confusion about the core consecration of religious life as such. Extrapolation of this functional change by various theologians then redefined the entire meaning and import of religious consecration by public, perpetual vow.[24] The theological context for the relationship among common life, poverty, obedience, chastity, and ministry was reduced to a historical, outdated imposition, while unverifiable popular explanations engendered immense misunderstanding among religious (and

23   Ibid., 339–48.
24   Significant changes in the theological bases of religious life were also introduced by Elizabeth Johnson, C.S.J., who wrote the theological monograph for the sociological study (commonly known as FORUS) conducted by David Nygren, C.M., and Miriam Ukeritis, C.S.J. The study was funded by the Lilly Foundation, with its findings published in 1993 as *The Future of Religious Orders in the United States* (Westport, Conn.: Praeger, 1993). In Johnson's theological monograph titled "Between the Times: Religious Life and the Postmodern Experience of God," *Review for Religious* 53, no. 1 (January–February 1994): 6–28, she wrote, 23–24: "If there is a God at all, then this is absolute holy mystery that can never be fathomed. . . . This mystery does not dwell in isolation from the world but encompasses it as the Matrix of its being and becoming. *God in the world and the world in God—panentheism describes the mutual relation*" [emphasis added]. In concluding, Johnson notes that "*this* God" [original emphasis] is now "a key theological factor shaping the future of religious life in America." It is important to note that fundamental truths of the Catholic faith cannot be sustained by the tenets of process philosophy on which Johnson bases her theology of panentheism.

most everyone else in the Church) about what religious vows were really about. Again, my Dominican perspective regarding consecration by vow concerns the theological basis for who we are as religious and what we do as religious in the Church. Indeed, if those of us who profess vows as religious cannot even get our basic theology of religious life straight, then we are never going to get the basics of our life as religious straight. Unfortunately, this apparently small, mostly unnoticed, purely functional change in the order of the vows has actually cast a long shadow of theological confusion on the renewal of religious life.

Curial Oversight and Episcopal Vigilance

Post-conciliar overload at the Curia also unfortunately contributed indirectly to the transition of the (then) Conference of Major Religious Superiors of Women's Institutes (CMSW) into the Leadership Conference of Women Religious (LCWR) from 1967 to 1971. Despite multiple complaints, the Curia mostly overlooked the far-reaching consequences of LCWR's Sisters' Survey project, begun in 1965, which used sociological methods and less-than-verifiable "belief scales." The Sisters' Survey was based on the 1963 doctoral dissertation in sociology of Sister Marie Augusta Neal, S.N.D.deN., which had been explicitly designed to assess readiness for change in a random sample of 259 Boston diocesan clergy.[25] But, for the 139,691 women religious who completed the twenty-three-page booklet of 649 questions, the Sisters' Survey itself functioned as a "change agent" by reason of the content alone. LCWR executives assessed the Sisters' Survey as being "catalytic far beyond what its creators dreamed,"[26] while Neal herself admitted that the "pre-and-

25 Marie Augusta Neal, S.N.D.deN., *Values and Interests in Social Change* (Englewood Cliffs, N.J.: Prentice Hall, 1965).

26 Quiñonez and Turner, *The Transformation of American Catholic Sisters,* 43–44, note that the research project that became the Sisters' Survey was conceived by "several American sisters" who met "at Grailville, Ohio, in 1964" and "gained access to an advance draft of the Vatican II document on religious life." The Sisters' Survey project, approved in 1965, "directly affected the initial organization of change in women's communities" and "was instrumental in enabling chapters to see clearly the task a community faced in living

post-Vatican II belief scales . . . became the most controversial and the most discriminating variable, which accounted for the pace and direction of changes in structures of the religious congregations involved."[27] Nor did the (then) Congregation for Religious and Secular Institutes seem much alarmed when Marie Augusta Neal reported to that dicastery in her June 1969 "Memo" on survey results that "there is a proneness to fascism in the sister who prefers a pre-Vatican belief orientation."[28]

Simultaneously, multiple change-oriented general chapters influenced by the Sisters' Survey, in conjunction with a parallel lack of curial oversight and of appropriate curial intervention, provided the context for communities to initiate open placement in apostolates and apostolic invisibility in attire. These changes brought institutional decline and emergence of "communities" wherein sisters related occasionally while living alone instead of living in common. Ongoing renewal chapters also eroded the legal stability of congregations as "leadership teams" replaced superiors and councils, as chapters became large volunteer assemblies controlled by appointed-outside-facilitators, and as those in "leadership" began "governing" through multiple levels of administrative appointees.

Also, in the first twenty years after Vatican II, when a member of the hierarchy occasionally intervened in matters related to women religious, it usually became an immediate media cause célèbre for those in progressive communities while simultaneously becoming an embarrassment for traditional-oriented sisters in these communities, as well as for many Catholic faithful. From the Los Angeles I.H.M. confrontation in the late 1960s, to the resignation from public

---

into . . . a new paradigm, of religious life" (48–49). The 1965 book, *The Changing Sister* (see n. 14 above) also emerged from this 1964 Grailville meeting (44). Recall that Turner and Quiñonez were sequentially executive directors of LCWR from 1972 to 1986.

27 Neal, *From Nuns to Sisters*, 126–27n9.

28 From the unpublished June 1969 "Memo" of Marie Augusta Neal to the Congregation for Religious and Secular Institutes. Portions of the "Memo" appear in the doctoral dissertation of M. M. Modde, O.S.F., *A Canonical Study of the LCWR* (Washington, D.C.: The Catholic University of America Press, 1977), 126–28. The "Memo" can still be found in archives of some religious communities (which is where this author's copy was obtained). See also, Elizabeth McDonough, O.P., "The Sisters' Survey Revisited," *Review for Religious* 63, no. 4 (2004): 387–401, especially 393–97.

office and departure from religious life in 1983 of Sister Agnes Mary Mansour, R.S.M., to the *New York Times* ad of October 1984, confrontation escalated between bishops and some individual religious or some religious institutes until the Quinn Commission reported in the mid-1980s that religious life in the USA was basically "in good condition."[29] What happened, however, was that the ongoing, functional tutelage of LCWR had successfully brought community after community entirely within the control of progressive leadership who belonged to that conference, which systematically co-opted the entire course of renewal by effecting a "corporate transformation" into a liberal-feminist-ecological-social-justice-oriented agenda.[30] Meanwhile, bishops became increasingly wary of any intervention regarding women religious even in matters pertaining to diocesan communities. Many bishops readily (but erroneously) claimed they had no authority whatsoever regarding pontifical religious institutes. After twenty years of sporadic confrontation culminating during the time when LCWR successfully co-opted the Quinn Commission's assessment,[31] the hierarchy adopted a deliberate "Gamaliel" approach to the growing problem of the renewal of religious life in the United States, particularly regarding communities of women religious.[32]

29   See n. 7 above.

30   Quiñonez and Turner, *The Transformation of American Catholic Sisters,* "Changing Times," 3–30. Along with its name, LCWR's mission changed radically from 1967 to 1971 and accomplished the "transformation" praised in their book. See 18 and 23: "The evolution of the LCWR's perception of its own mission is an important index of a changing self-definition" and "The striking redirection of the conference's mission did not take place without struggle." See 164: "Sisters are not the only ones in the last three decades who have been schooled in change and conflict. However, theirs is a corporate transformation." And see 165–67, "Afterward." Co-option of the renewal asked of religious by Vatican II is still evident even in the USCCB's National Religious Retirement Office. The November 2007 "LCWR Update" reports that Sandra Schneiders offered "theological insights on the future of religious life," and Ruby Cribbins, a facilitator for reconfigurations, "brought her perspective" at an October 2007 meeting held after the NRRO board decided more national collection funds would be allotted to "systemic change."

31   For examples of LCWR's involvement in the Quinn Commission process, see Quiñonez and Turner, *The Transformation of American Catholic Sisters,* 86–87, and Carey, *Sisters in Crisis,* 225–26. (See also nn. 7 and 15 above).

32   Carey, *Sisters in Crisis,* 227–28 and 231–32, notes and comments on the recommendation that bishops adopt the "Gamaliel Principle" (Acts 5:34–39) and simply let trends in religious life in the United States continue on their course without intervention by members of the hierarchy. In late March 1989, Pope John Paul II wrote to the bishops

Thereafter, more communities and their apostolic endeavors continued to gravitate toward being global business organizations in structure and orientation. Leadership teams, functioning primarily in corporate executive lifestyles, redefined congregational charisms in terms of global mission requiring internal restructuring. They then initiated multiple corporate mergers referred to as "reconfigurations," which are still occurring.[33] All along, perhaps because of the "Gamaliel Principle," vigilance and oversight by the hierarchy were most evident by their absence. From the clearer perspective of hindsight, the genuine "losers" in this escalating trend are: (1) nonprogressive sisters "caught" in progressive communities with no ability to alter the direction and agendas set by their "leadership teams"; (2) senior sisters who suffer a never-imagined experience of radical, inner poverty; (3) Catholic faithful who wonder, "Where have all the Sisters gone?" as community assets are depleted by deliberate divestiture of immovable assets[34] or by a corporate executive lifestyle among leadership who—along with members—publicly challenge fundamentals of Catholic belief and practice but are apparently not held to any internal or external accountability; and (4) the immensely significant genuine religious heritage of the entire Catholic Church in the United States, which is fast disappearing from (perhaps) not-so-benign neglect.

The thousands of nonprogressive sisters who are literally "caught" in progressive communities in the United States and who have had no realistic opportunity to live the renewal asked of them constitute both a personal and an ecclesial tragedy of immense proportion as

who had met with him earlier that month to discuss the final Quinn Commission Report. In this communication, he addressed "tendencies to excessive self-fulfillment and autonomy of living, working and decision-making, community life and vowed life," adding that past abuses of authority in religious institutes did not warrant "substitution of a management model of authority for a government model as the answer." He also commented that, because religious are "public persons in the church, their own obligation . . . is to reflect accurately and clearly the teaching of the church." *Origins* (April 19, 1989): 745–48.

33   See nn. 2 and 9 above.

34   For example, the Benedictine Sisters of Wisconsin, assisted by Rev. Daniel Ward, O.S.B., JD, JCL, gradually transferred monastery property to themselves, eventually requested and received dispensations from their vows, and then began an ecumenical center on the same property. See Robert McClory, "Ecumenical Monastery in Wisconsin Charts a New Way," *National Catholic Reporter* (August 17, 2007): 10–11.

well as a genuine *de agendo* that has rendered the renewal of religious life mandated by Vatican II as mostly never really tried at all.[35] Our senior sisters now see the efforts of generations evaporating before their eyes as they move to retirement facilities with sisters from multiple, merged congregations who have little in common except claiming the same charism and having the same letters after their names. Faithful, hard-working laity who financed the Church's educational and hospital systems established and operated successfully by women religious for two centuries now see these institutions closed or operated by laity or sold and used as for-profit entities, even as the laity are now asked to finance our senior sisters' retirement. And it is possible that part of our nation's Catholic heritage—integral to its *institutio Christiana* and *regula fidei* and to the support of its *lex orandi* and *lex credendi* and *lex vivendi*—is in genuine jeopardy from a long-term failure to recognize that what occurred in renewing religious life in the United States may (mostly) not be what Vatican II asked of us at all. Religious in progressive communities who are not themselves progressive sensed this long ago. Now they sense a very limited ability to alter current agendas.

In short, during the four-plus decades since Vatican II, some of us who are religious seem to have made some very serious mistakes in interpreting and implementing that Council. Some in positions erroneously labeled as "leadership" have apparently failed to meet multiple moral and legal and spiritual obligations entrusted to them by members of their own communities. Some among the hierarchy seem at times to have forgotten their obligation to exercise genuine, responsible vigilance—as successors of the apostles—regarding the public role of religious in the dioceses entrusted to their care as well as in the universal Church. However, all of the above may now be changing because of renewed interest and effort on the part of sisters and major superiors and members of the hierarchy to be more aware of and to better understand and to respond in meaningful, measured fashion to the realities of religious life today that greatly concern us all.

35   *De agendo* is the technical, theological term for evil, understood as lack of some good that should be present.

Between the Idea and the Reality

If we are at all honest from the perspective of hindsight spanning some twenty years of conflict and twenty years of compromise in implementing the renewal initiated by Vatican II, those of us who are religious might have to admit we are not so much renewed as we would like to think. We might also have to admit that religious life in the United States has hardly experienced the renewal some may try to claim. Whether this perspective reflects forty years of hindsight or forty years of endurance or (perhaps) both, it certainly reveals a visible, veritable chasm between two groups of women religious in this country. On one side of this chasm are those who seem to have trod a circuitous path of unchecked adaptation leading to the brink of imminent extinction. On the other side are those who seem to have trod a straight road of studiously maintaining a very respectable *status quo ante*. The latter are not likely to disappear, not merely because this form of life is genuinely attractive to the new generation of youth, but because in every transition from one dominant form of religious life to another (monasticism, mendicants, apostolic congregations, etc.) the prior form did not simply disappear, if it still had something significant to offer to the great diversity of the truly universal Catholic Church. Also, within progressive communities in the United States, there is a far less visible but no less real chasm between sisters who espouse or follow the current, progressive agendas favored by leadership and those who desire to live more faithfully the vows they thought they once professed. No matter which side of these great external or internal religious-life chasms one favors or on which side of these great chasms one may happen to be, consequences of what Vatican II asked of us have left women religious still—to some extent—wandering in a forty-year desert with multiple mirages of self-proclaimed progress toward what appears to be an ever-elusive promised land of "authentic renewal."

Looking to the future with the enhanced clarity of more than four decades of hindsight, the underlying realities and related challenges of implementing Vatican II's call to renewal are ongoing. We still know not where this all might lead as we are called to grow daily in a deeper embrace of living the reality that God must eventually, truly and totally, become our "enough." And no matter what transpires, we are each still and always called to ongoing, generous fidelity to the promise each of us once made—freely, joyfully, generously—to give our very self to God alone, forever. God is faithful, and it is God who will see to it that all manner of things shall eventually be well.

Four

Signs of the Times

Signs, Symbols, and Meaning in Religious Life

JOSEPH T. LIENHARD, S.J.

In the film *Into Great Silence,* recorded at the Grande Chartreuse in the French Alps, a fascinating sequence takes place. In the segment entitled "Dinner," the monks are filing into the refectory. But before they enter, they hold their hands under a little running water and then dry them on a roll-towel. Since the day is a feast day, recreation outdoors follows dinner. At the recreation, a conversation takes place. These are the words spoken:

"In Sélignac they have not been washing their hands before the refectory for twenty years now."

"Do you think we should stop washing our hands?"

"No, but it wouldn't be a big deal to get rid of something useless."

"Our entire life, the whole liturgy, and everything ceremonial are symbols."

"If you tear down the symbols, then you tear down the walls of your own house."

"In the monastery in Pavia, instead of one wash-basin they have six. There you can wash your hands properly."

"Yes, they're also Trappists."

"When we abolish the signs, we lose our orientation. Instead, we should search for their meaning."

"But one should unfold the core of the symbols."

"The signs are not to be questioned, we are."

"I'm not against hand washing. I just forget to dirty my hands first."

"The error is not to be found in hand washing, the error is in our mind."

This dialogue encapsulates the crisis that has plagued religious life for forty years. The crisis concerns signs, symbols, and meaning. The hand washing is a sign, a symbol. Should the monks abolish the symbol as useless? Is it merely functional, to clean dirty hands? Is there a meaning behind the symbol? Can you preserve the meaning and abolish the symbol?

Ten Theses for Renewal

This essay addresses the significance of signs, symbols, and their meaning in apostolic religious life using ten specific theses.

1   *A sign is a thing known first that leads to knowledge of another thing. Signs may be natural or conventional.*

Perhaps in the first class of the treatise on sacraments, religious learned about signs: things known first that lead to knowledge of other things. Natural signs communicate knowledge of what they signify by their very nature: inevitably, the example of a natural sign is smoke, which leads to knowledge that there is fire below it. Conventional signs gain their meaning from agreement among the users of the sign: letters of the alphabet are one example; the national flag is another. By its nature, a rectangle of cloth with red and white stripes, and a blue field with white stars in one corner, has no intrinsic meaning; but it has a great deal of meaning for those who agree to that meaning.

2 *Symbols are natural signs to which further signification has been added by the one who instituted them.*

Symbols stand between natural signs and conventional signs: they are natural signs to which further signification has been added by the one who instituted them. One example of symbols is sacraments: water cleanses, bread and wine nourish; but, by the will of Christ, the water of baptism and the bread and wine of the Eucharist mean much more than simple cleansing or nourishing.

3 *Almost from the beginning, religious life has had a set of signs and symbols that express meaning. These signs and symbols communicated their meaning to the religious themselves, to the other members of the religious community, and to those outside the community.*

Without undertaking a history of religious life, it is clear historically that in the second, third, and fourth centuries the ascetical life existed before monasticism. From the second or third century on, there is evidence of "family ascetics": often enough, women who practiced asceticism but continued to live with their families. Their characteristics were celibacy or virginity, restrained diet, and prayer, all of these understood as a kind of self-offering. These characteristics already functioned as signs. Asceticism became monasticism when the ascetics separated themselves from the rest of the Christian community and lived apart—either as hermits, or in groups of hermits, or in a community. Antony and the many other monks described in the *Apophthegmata patrum* and so much other literature from the fourth and fifth centuries had much in common: simple dress, restrained diet, extensive prayer, even if the practices were voluntary. These practices were signs or symbols of religious dedication. A significant change began with Pachomius and the monasticism of the upper Nile. One might say that Pachomius made religious life accessible to the mediocre. The primary virtue was no longer ascetical achievement, but obedience. Pachomius's monks were to live a highly structured life, a life of prayer, work, and reading or instruction. And in cenobitic monasticism the number and importance of signs increased.

4   *The principal signs of religious life in a community were uniform clothing or the habit,*[1] *common residence, common table, similar furnishings, common Mass and prayer, and a horarium or daily order.*

The general outline of the monastic life that Pachomius established is fairly well known.[2] Each monk had his own cell; cells were in houses of twenty or more monks each. At dawn a gong or horn called the monks to prayer, which consisted of reading from the Scripture and recitation of the Lord's Prayer, with periods of silence. The monks worked with their hands during the prayer. Only on days when the Eucharist was celebrated did they sing or pray psalms. After prayer, the day's work was organized. Work assignments changed each week. Dress was a tunic with a belt, a goatskin and hood over the shoulders, boots, and perhaps a staff. The monks had two meals a day: the main meal during the working period and a lighter meal in the evening. The gong was sounded, and all ate together. The meal consisted of bread and cooked vegetables. After the evening meal, the monks sometimes received the *tragematia,* perhaps a dessert of dried fruit, which they could take to their houses and which was supposed to last for three days. In the evening, there was a period of instruction and prayer, and prayers in each house before the monks retired.

Religious can recognize some elements of their tradition in this short description of life in a Pachomian monastery. There are, after all, only a finite number of ways to live life in a community. One might argue that the elements of religious life were, from the beginning, simply pragmatic, without any further signification as signs or symbols, as the Carthusian who wanted proper hand washing for dirty hands implied. But I would argue the opposite. The monks' simple, uniform dress communicated a message to those who saw

1   Uniform clothing was not a Christian innovation. In the pagan world, for example, a philosopher was recognized by his dress, and different styles of dress were prescribed for different classes of men in Rome.

2   This section is taken, often verbatim, from Philip Rousseau, *Pachomius: The Making of a Community in Fourth-Century Egypt,* Transformation of the Classical Heritage 6 (Berkeley: University of California Press, 1985).

it, and also to the monks themselves. A century or so later, the dark cloaks of Saint Augustine and his companions would communicate a similar message. The common table, the daily order, the rotating work assignments, all communicated a deeper meaning to the monks themselves: equality, charity, the conviction that this life is the means to an end beyond itself.

5   *No one of the signs just mentioned is essential to religious life.*

The signs mentioned in the account of Pachomian monasticism recur with consistent regularity throughout the history of religious life. But it is also possible to trace the abandonment of some of these signs as religious life changed. The most noticeable change in religious life, and one that came gradually, was the change from monastic stability and the contemplative life to an apostolic, mobile, and active life. A brief sketch will illustrate this point.

Over the centuries in the West, there was a gradual move from monastic stability to active ministry (a move never taken by Byzantine monasticism, despite Saint Basil of Caesarea's preference for some apostolate for his monks). Both religious leaders and secular rulers saw monks, or religious, as a potential work force. Gregory the Great sent Roman monks to England as missionaries. Charlemagne wanted monks to tame the central European wilderness. The Cistercians opened up new territory for settlement. By the sixteenth century, religious were ready to go as missionaries to the newly discovered lands of the western hemisphere and of Africa.

The habit became more stylized, perhaps, with the rise of Benedictine monasteries, and certainly more distinctive and differentiated with the rise of the canons regular in the twelfth century and of the mendicant orders in the thirteenth.

Another, dramatic change took place with the rise of the mendicants: a new style of residence, convents that a religious might move into and then leave to live in another convent. Monks had vowed stability, remaining in one monastery for life; the mendicants were men on the move. As the economy of Europe developed and expanded, beginning around the eleventh century, a merchant class arose that was mobile, and new cities were founded. Monasteries were often out in the countryside. In some cases, cities grew up around monasteries; Munich is an example. In more cases, though, the mendicants, with their urban parishes and convents, used their mobility to serve the spiritual needs of the city-dwellers, providing sacramental life, devotions, pious associations, and other forms of spiritual life for the urban population.

In the sixteenth century, the Jesuits made another shift, and one that gave rise to strong objections: namely, the abandonment of choir. The Jesuits also gave up a common habit; they were to wear the dress of good priests of the area.

In times of stress or persecution, as during the French Revolution or the anticlerical regime in Mexico, religious dress and life in community might be abandoned altogether. Sometimes, too, congregations adopted a form of dress like that of secular people of the time, on the grounds that it gave them increased apostolic effectiveness. My home parish in New York had a convent of the Parish Visitors of Mary Immaculate, who had adopted a kind of conservative secular dress in the 1920s, and kept it: by the 1950s the sisters looked like 1920s flappers in black, with cloche hats and black dresses.

It is important to repeat: no one sign is essential to religious life. For various reasons—usually either apostolic mobility or apostolic ministry—orders in the past abandoned one or other of the signs of religious life. Sometimes, too, religious had to abandon most of the signs of consecrated life simply to survive.

6   *Although religious life had suffered setbacks in the past, the abandonment of signs, beginning around 1965, was unprecedented, both in the extent to which signs were abandoned and in the fact that the abandonment came from within religious life.*

Throughout its history, religious life suffered setbacks from outside—for example, the Reformation in the sixteenth century, or the Secularization in the late eighteenth and early nineteenth centuries. Religious life also suffered decay and collapse from within; many of the monasteries that were secularized in the early nineteenth century were mere shells of their former selves, and observance had fallen off drastically. When a religious order declines and dies, it usually does so because of the abandonment of poverty and common life. History also attests to more than a few reforms of religious orders from within: Benedictines, Franciscans, Carmelites, and Cistercians are the most obvious examples.

A few examples drawn largely from personal experience show how various signs were abandoned and what negative results followed. Beginning around 1965, in an unprecedented move, religious undertook the abandonment of signs, voluntarily and even enthusiastically. Religious or clerical dress was abandoned, and secular dress was adopted, on the grounds that it would bring religious closer to the people. (A Jesuit who works on a university campus on which the Jesuits have abandoned clerical dress was recently quoted as saying, "Nobody knows who we are. We should get T-shirts or sweatshirts or something." What might that "something" be?) Having buffet meals rather than a common dinner would make us more apostolically available; but common grace and common visits to the Blessed Sacrament after dinner disappeared along with the common meal. With the abandonment of the horarium, morning visit and night visit disappeared. For a while, it seemed that the answer to anyone's problem was to move out of the community into an apartment. Religious began to have checking accounts, and they depended less and less on the community for clothing, furniture, or recreation. Vacations together evaporated, as members took private vacations or went off in small, self-selecting groups.

The examples given are not wholesale; since the 1960s and 1970s, there has been some self-correction. What has not taken place, however, is serious reflection on the meaning of the signs and symbols that marked religious life.

7 *Existence without signs—that is, the attempt to communicate meaning or reality without signs—is impossible.*

On the most basic level, apostolic religious must acknowledge that it is impossible, in this life, to have meaning without signs. Communication depends on signs, the most basic of which are words. We are always communicating, and hence we are always using signs. Even the Holy Scriptures are a sign. In an extraordinarily beautiful paragraph, Saint Augustine described how the Scriptures will not be needed in the Beatific Vision:

> When our Lord Jesus Christ has come, . . . lamps will not be necessary. A prophet will not be read to us, the book of the Apostle will not be opened; we shall not seek the testimony of John, we shall not need the Gospel itself. Therefore, all the Scriptures will be taken from our midst which were burning as lamps for us in the night of this world that we might not remain in the darkness.[3]

Humanity, however, has not yet reached this state of blessedness. On a far more mundane level, life in community is a sign, too; and like all signs, it always communicates some meaning, if not always the right one. For example, the five-year-old nephew of a friend visited our community. He saw a group of men living together without women. His five-year-old mind, seeking a category to interpret this sign, concluded that we were cowboys.

8   *When religious rejected or abandoned common or historical signs, they did not live without signs but adopted new ones.*

As already pointed out, some religious in the past abandoned the habit, often in times of stress; others never had a habit. Some were forced to live apart from communities, often for a high ideal, such as missionaries. The customary signs of religious life might be abandoned, but we cannot live without signs. Once common signs are abandoned, other signs step in to take their place—in many cases, signs that divide rather than unite. Father A wears neckties to work, Father B wears a clerical collar. Each thinks he's right, and hence (by implication, at least) that the other is wrong. Sister C wears simple, dark-colored—albeit secular—clothing, and no jewelry; Sister D has some brightly colored, stylish clothing and several pairs of fine earrings. In each case, a sign is pointing to a reality beyond itself: the question is, which reality?

---

3   *Tractates on John,* 35, 9, trans. John W. Rettig, in *St. Augustine: Tractactates on the Gospel of John 28–54,* Fathers of the Church 88 (Washington, D.C.: The Catholic University of America Press, 1993), 79.

9 *The new signs often pointed to secularity, disunity, and comfort.*

Perhaps it's a distinctly American trait, but religious here seem eager to make their lives better, more comfortable. The sets of signs that some individual religious or communities have adopted send a clear message to the community and to the world outside the community. Perhaps religious need to stop and ask what that message is.

10 *Appropriate reform or progress will probably not be achieved by restoration of the (poorly remembered) past, but by rigorous reform and the establishment of a renewed set of common signs and symbols.*

Since this tenth and last thesis concerns the future, it is impossible to comment on it. However, it does contain a question all religious need to ask.

Conclusion

In short, what is the point of this essay? First, religious employ signs and symbols because they facilitate communication. A sign is not only a thing known first, but a thing known more easily and more quickly. In traffic signs, the meaning of the horizontal bar is perceived more quickly than the words "One Way—Do Not Enter." Perhaps the veil or the habit does the same thing.

In religious life, there are both signs and symbols. The fact that all the members of a teaching community live in the same size rooms, no matter what their position or salary, is a sign. The brown cassock and the rope belt is a symbol, a sign with additional meaning assigned to it by the founder.

To live religious life without signs and symbols is impossible. We are sign-makers and live in a world of signs. Of course, it is possible to have signs without signification, as one might see in a dying monastery. What happened in the past forty years or so is not the abolition of signs but the dissolution of common signs. Often in the name of apostolic service or availability, common signs were rejected. Work, for example, would always excuse a religious from prayer, Mass, or a meal. The result was not an absence of signs but a new set of signs that separated or divided rather than unified. A community without common signs often lost the meaning that those signs were meant to express.

In other words, sign and thing signified are intimately connected. At least since the Fall, signs are necessary to communication—language is only the most obvious example. For religious to think that they can exist or flourish without the signs of religious life and community life is a form of angelism.

In conclusion, I have no formula that will solve the problem I have raised. I doubt that brute restorationism is the answer. But all religious know of some orders that are flourishing and others that are dying. "Liberal" and "conservative" are generally not helpful analytical categories; they stop action and reflection rather than encourage it. Rather than speaking of liberal or conservative orders, we might find some other criterion for evaluating them. I have suggested that religious should reflect on their lives in terms of signs, symbols, and signification. Perhaps apostolic religious are on the way to some new insight. But one thing is certain: as the Carthusian monk said, "If you tear down the symbols, then you tear down the walls of your own house."

Five

Relearning the Language of God

Obedience, Forgiveness, and Love

BISHOP ROBERT MORLINO

Listening, watching, and reading media reports these days, in terms of the recent economic crisis in the United States, we find that one particular power group suggests that the plan proposed is a "bailout"; a bailout for the wealthy and the greedy—that doesn't sound very good. Another group says that it's a "rescue plan" for the tax payer—that sounds very good. Which is it? Is it a bailout or is it a rescue? Is it negative or is it positive? This is known as "spin." What the representatives of these different power groups are trying to do, by repeating it over and over again, is to teach others a *language.* Some want the country to speak the language of "rescue"; others want society to speak the language of "bailout." They are trying to teach a new language; people learn language by repetition. An awful lot of money is being spent, so certain political figures can repeat regularly, what they repeat, and teach society a new language. When someone is trying to teach a new language, repetition obviously works. There is nothing new about that. As Saint Ignatius

Loyola said, *repetitio est mater studiorum:* it's the only way to learn.

The sentiments expressed by Cardinal Rodé in his essay in this volume give one hope regarding the future of religious life. I could not be more in agreement with his concrete recommendations, especially regarding formation and continuing education. Since the Second Vatican Council people have been taught a language, but people, especially middle-aged people, need to learn a new language. In the case of people my age, it's really profoundly difficult, because they have to *unlearn* a language, one with which they have become very familiar since the Second Vatican Council.

A good illustration of the difficulty with language is my own challenge to learn Spanish. I can read Spanish, but I cannot speak it, because I have to *unlearn* Italian, in order to do so. Today, it's more important for me to speak Spanish than Italian. But for me Italian is more habitual. So, it's very difficult for me to speak Spanish, without defaulting to Italian, each time I pause to take a breath.

It's very hard to learn a new language, if we have to *unlearn* another language to do so. Since Vatican II the language that many have learned is that of the discontinuity hermeneutic, the language of rupture between pre–Vatican II and post–Vatican II. As expressed in the essays herein, a new language about the Church and religious life arose after Vatican II. Clearly the new language has not worked well, as evidenced by the state of religious life in the United States today.

It is necessary, therefore, to listen to the language offered by recent popes. But in order to learn the language that Pope John Paul the Great and Pope Benedict are trying to teach us, we must unlearn the language that we learned. That's very difficult, and I try to remind myself every morning in prayer how difficult it is to unlearn a language, because I seemingly cannot unlearn Italian in order to speak Spanish. Thus, I truly sympathize with those who are called to unlearn a language, in order to learn the one needed. However, the reality remains that religious need a new language in order to follow the correct interpretation of Vatican II, as they move toward the future. This language is needed by all, but especially for younger people, including sisters, priests, and seminarians, because they are not battle-hardened the way some older religious are. It would be better for their spiritual formation not to face the daily experience of battle; that's a hard way to wake up every morning. Like all good fathers and mothers, we want to leave our spiritual sons and daughters, our spiritual grandsons and granddaughters, a better sense of life in Christ, and in the Church, than we experienced.

Some reflection on language taught to older religious is essential. In essence religious life comes down to obedience. Poverty is an instance of obedience, when you live the religious life; it is obedience to a particular rule or constitution. Celibacy, celibate chastity, is an instance of obedience to the call of Jesus Christ, to sacrifice marriage for the sake of the Kingdom. The eschatological witness that we are called to live is an instance of obedience. Prayer, the daily structured prayer life, is an instance of obedience. Why is that so? It is because Jesus became obedient unto death, even death on a cross. The author of the Letter to the Hebrews (5:8) says Jesus learned obedience from what he suffered. In the Garden of Gethsemane, Jesus said, "Not my will Father, but thy will be done" (Mt 26:39c). Saint Paul says Jesus was never at one moment *yes* and another moment *no* to his Father; Jesus was never anything but yes (2 Cor 1:18). So, Jesus' sacrificial death on the cross, that act of love, was in fact an act of obedience, and an act of forgiveness.

One way to sum up this idea is in the form of a simple equation: Obedience + Forgiveness = Love = Charity. But what happened? Obedience was reduced, it was redefined, and it was spun as an autonomous act that is justified by following one's conscience.

Today the word "deconstruct" is often heard with respect to religious life. In 1968, at the time of *Humanae Vitae,* the word "conscience" was deconstructed. Conscience was separated from its focus on discovering the objective truth. Conscience is a creature; it is not the creator of truth. Conscience is subject to the truth received from Scripture and tradition, as interpreted by the magisterium. The Holy Father and the bishops have something to do with people maintaining a right, rather than an erroneous, conscience. If people have an erroneous conscience, they still have to follow it, but that can't be the end of the story. If people who have an erroneous conscience do not see the Holy Father and the bishops as speaking to that erroneous conscience, then they are not in the Catholic Church. In such a case conscience becomes the creator of the moral law, rather than the creature, a human faculty, that is meant to latch on and discover the moral law. *Humanae Vitae* "took the lid off," in terms of the deconstruction of the word "conscience." Conscience became supreme. This is not to say that artificial contraception is at the root of every other problem; rather artificial contraception caused the deconstruction of the word "conscience" on a widespread level among Catholics. Catholics felt perfectly free to dissent and to "follow their conscience," and they were consistent enough to know that if they could follow their conscience with regard to *Humanae Vitae,* they could follow their conscience with regard to anything else. This was the beginning of the malaise of religious life, because conscience was no longer a creature, but creator of the truth and free to reduce, to redefine, to deconstruct. Conscience so redefined deconstructed obedience to be some kind of consensus activity lead by a facilitator, rather than imitating Jesus Christ, by sacrificing the intellect and will completely, in obedience to superiors and lawful authority in the Church. Obedience got deconstructed because conscience saw obedience differently than the tradition of the Church.

Then, conscience took on poverty, which was reduced to getting permission. In the late sixties and the seventies it meant little else. Thus, poverty basically went out of existence, not in every case, but institutionally/structurally, because poverty was reduced to obedience. If I got permission, I kept my vow of poverty. All that was required in those days was to go to the superior and use the word "discern." If you said to the superior, "I discerned this," you got permission. And if you got permission, you kept the vow of poverty. That's a kind of profound reductionism. I used to joke with my friends who seemed to conjugate the verb "discern": I discern, you discern, I decide, when we should be conjugating it: I discern, you discern, He (God) decides. Poverty was reduced to obedience.

Celibate chastity was reduced to the abstention from the physical expression of sex. Celibacy, which is God's special gift to religious and to priests, is the sacrifice of marriage for the sake of the

Kingdom of God—the *sacrifice* of marriage: one husband, one wife, one lifetime, openness to children, wanting to be a great dad, wanting to be a great husband. Jesus gives some the grace to sacrifice spouse, children, and the desire to be a good parent. Celibacy is not just a matter of abstaining from the physical expression of sex. Celibacy has to do with what I *think* and what I *feel* when I'm abstaining. There is no mind-body split. Today's culture wants to redefine marriage. But if you redefine marriage, you need to redefine celibacy. That's what I mean by spin and playing with words. The redefinition of marriage is particularly perilous for the Church. All of the connections are beyond the scope of this essay, but so much of what we believe depends on the definition of marriage that we have, from Christ, through the Scriptures, in the Church. If marriage is redefined, the ripple effect of that decision will be something worse than the ripple effect of our current economic situation, which remains unknown. But in order to be the Church of Jesus Christ and to love him, we need to know what marriage is. If marriage can be redefined in the minds of people, celibacy will have to be redefined. However, marriage cannot be redefined. Society cannot sit back and watch the redefinition of marriage happen, for all people of faith have a great stake in such a change.

Thus, obedience, poverty, and celibate chastity got deconstructed; the eschatological witness of religious life was basically set aside in favor of liberation theology. Some religious chose to be messianic and perfect this world, rather than being focused on the world to come, as should be the role of religious. Prayer was reduced to looking at different options and variations. This too became a matter of conscience; if I follow my conscience I am as "good as gold." Conscience becomes the key to the false freedom of disobedience. While humanity proves its freedom by disobedience, Jesus proves his freedom by obedience, most especially his act of obedience on the cross.

Without the replication of Christ's act of obedience in the Church, day in and day out, we cannot really be the body of Christ. Thus, when religious life is deconstructed, redefined, or reduced, this is a more serious crisis than the recent economic crisis, because not only is this a crisis that pertains to money in time, but it's a crisis that pertains to salvation in eternity.

Obedience + Forgiveness = Love. At Mass Catholics have the act of obedience of Jesus Christ, his one eternal sacrifice to the Father. We are able to be present to that act of obedience, that one eternal sacrifice. We are able to join in and sacrifice ourselves, through poverty, chastity, obedience, eschatological witness, and prayer. We are called to sacrifice ourselves with Christ, in Christ, through Christ, in that one eternal sacrificial "moment" in heaven. Jesus offered that act of obedience, so that there might be mercy, so that there might be forgiveness. So, too in the Mass the faithful are pulled into "Obedience + Forgiveness = Love." The forgiveness aspect of this act is very important. Earlier, I mentioned some religious waking up in the morning after the past forty years, feeling embattled or under siege. Some religious are angry about that. It wouldn't make sense for them to be happy about it, but some are downright angry about it.

Religious must forgive the harsh reality of life in the Church during the past forty years. They should not pass over or overlook it. They cannot say, "Oh, let's move on." They must face the fact that, for the past forty years, life in the Church has been harsh, but there is a need to forgive that reality from the heart; otherwise there will be no peace or joy in moving on. Over the past forty years, many religious have felt like losers, while others were winners. There can be no joy for some in making others feel like losers, while they feel like winners. There are *only* winners in Christ; there are *no* losers.

Thus, we must truly reflect, pray, and forgive. When we think about formation and continuing formation for priests, brothers, and sisters, this element of forgiveness needs to be part of the equation. There's actually a department at the University of Wisconsin, Madison, called the Institute for Forgiveness. Students can earn a doctorate in forgiveness. It's a combination of psychology with solid underpinnings compatible with Catholic faith. If I had a concrete suggestion it would be that the need for forgiveness be incorporated fully into formation and continuing education. Religious must forgive the ecclesial reality of the past forty years, but it's probably less forgiveness than is needed in the ordinary marriage. With God's grace, religious can face this. Yes, obedience in Christ is required, but if religious want to have love, they need that forgiveness every bit as much.

The only other concrete recommendation I have is that the Church really needs to be careful concerning the education of novices for the consecrated life, or young seminarians or brothers for the religious life. Great care also has to be taken that formation and continuing formation include strong and clear instruction with regard to the natural law. Bishops need to be very careful about who speaks to priests for continuing education, or who is teaching the seminarians or candidates for religious life. When situations arise that compromise the catechetical mission of the bishop, then the ordinary must push back. Today this is seen more in terms of diocesan policy. I hope that the superiors of religious communities are being vigilant about guest speakers; it doesn't make sense for us to spend time and money promoting the discontinuity hermeneutic, while ongoing education does not extol a hermeneutic of continuity. Thus, I suggest concretely that bishops give great attention to speakers, and I would suggest most strongly that, however it is done, forgiveness be incorporated into the processes of continuing education. Let's incorporate forgiveness, so that apostolic religious life can go forward with peace and joy, where everyone in the Church is a winner, according to the mind of Christ.

.

*Part II. Religious Life and
the Renewal of Love*

Six

Love Alone Is Credible

GILL GOULDING, C.J.

Caritas Christi urget nos. This *cri de coeur* from St Paul is a help-ful reminder to focus our living and activity as religious men and women. Love alone makes us credible as religious—not our love, manufactured by our own efforts and will, but the love of Christ, deeply rooted in his relationship with the Father and empowered by the work of the Spirit.[1] It is this Trinitarian love that is the root and ground and heart of religious life. It is the beauty of this love that calls forth our vocations, that inspires all our activity, and that com-municates through our joyful witness the eternal hope of the Gospel and the reconciliation that God so desires for our fractured world. The title of this essay is "borrowed" from a book written by the great Swiss theologian Hans Urs von Balthasar. I purloined it because it seems to me that it succinctly summarizes the divine initiative and impetus at work within apostolic religious life when coherently lived

---

The title has been taken from Hans Urs von Balthasar, *Love Alone Is Credible,* trans. D. C. Schindler (San Francisco: Ignatius Press, 2004). Original German edition: *Glaubhaft is nur Liebe,* 1963.

   1   Cf. John 15:16.

out in contemplation and action. It is the love of God in action in the person of Christ that opens our hearts and minds to the reality of intimacy with our God. It is from this depth of Trinitarian intimacy that we draw the resources for a credibility of love for all with whom we live and work. It is the imperious nature of this love that it has the power to draw us beyond the destructive "political" polarized struggles with which we all too readily engage and the gentleness to disarm even those who have grown hardened. It can lead us to seek what is common to every religious vocation and charism—intimacy with the Lord and a sharing in his redemptive mission. Following the exceedingly helpful essay of Sister Sara Butler, which clearly sets out the current state of religious life and the challenges we face, this essay seeks to identify where the treasure of apostolic religious life lies and suggests ways to more fruitfully live from that foundation in an authentic ecclesial witness. The structure of this essay is in three parts, three "jewels": (1) to identify the love that underpins our initial vocation, (2) to highlight the love expressed in the paschal mystery and the importance of ongoing conversion in our lives, and (3) to focus on the love that is manifested in an ecclesial commitment. This is no sentimental love but a "tough" love, a committed love, a passionate love willing to bear the cost of belonging to our Lord and our individual religious families and at the service of the Church in the world. Throughout this paper I shall be drawing on the work of Hans Urs von Balthasar and also on my Ignatian heritage.

The Love That Underpins Our Vocation

The love that calls religious in their vocation is the same love that brought each one of us into being, that loved us into existence from all eternity. This is both the reality of our own lives and the reality of the witness that we are called to share with those with whom we live and work and all with whom we engage. Thus, as the Holy Father reminds us:

> [God] loved me first, before I myself could love at all. It was only because he knew me and loved me that I was made. So I was not thrown

into the world by some operation of chance, as Heidegger says and now have to do my best to swim around in this ocean of life, but I am preceded by a perception of me, an idea and a love of me. They are present in the ground of my being. . . . God is there first and loves me. And that is the trustworthy ground on which my life is standing and on which I myself can construct it.[2]

So important is this understanding for Pope Benedict that his first encyclical, *Deus Caritas Est,* elaborates the reality of "the love which God lavishes upon us and which we in turn must share with others."[3] It is in the light of this love that the vocational call is framed. The Lord reminds us of this prevenient love, which draws forth a response of love that waits upon the leading of the Lord's spirit. It is aware of the divine initiative that is always present before us; it is the sure ground on which we walk forth into the future. It is vital that we continue to spend contemplative time drawing from this source. The call to prayer is primary in all our endeavors. It is the only way in which our apostolate will be fruitful. It is the disciplined commitment to a relationship with the Lord that will empower all our activity. Balthasar considers prayer to be so important that he maintains "the Christian stands and falls with prayer."[4] How much more is this so for the apostolic religious.

The call of Christ implies a choice, primarily God's choice of the individual and then the human response that disposes the individual to enter more deeply into the mission of Christ. This human response is as it were a self-abandonment, characterized by an openness that enables the choosing of God's choice. Religious cannot be more free than to choose God's choice. In Balthasar's *The Christian State of Life* he makes clear that the primary call of human beings is the call to love, love of God and love of neighbor. This is an absolute call and admits of no exception.[5] This love is active. In-

---

2   Cardinal Joseph Ratzinger, *God and Man* (San Francisco: Ignatius Press, 2002), 26–27.

3   Pope Benedict XVI, *Deus Caritas Est* (Washington, DC: USCCB, 2006), 2.

4   Hans Urs von Balthasar, *Elucidations* (London: SPCK, 1971), 113.

5   Hans Urs von Balthasar, "We Are Here to Love—Love God and to Love Our Neighbor," in *The Christian State of Life* (San Francisco: Ignatius Press, 1983), 27.

deed, if there was not a dynamic outward action of love it would not be truly love.[6] At the heart of this love is the mystery of self-giving and, consequently, of "choice." If love is true, "it gives itself to God and human beings by an interior movement that is wholly proper to it. . . . Because it is compelled by no necessity, necessity and freedom are conjoined in it."[7]

True love is radically and fundamentally disposed to renounce everything so that all may be held in readiness for the first sign of the will of the beloved. In the *Spiritual Exercises* Saint Ignatius stresses the way in which the lover shares with the beloved.[8] Balthasar emphasizes that God's love for human beings is so strong and true that the whole world is a demonstration of God's unsurpassing love. The particular call that religious have heard as individuals in a uniquely personal manner, through prayer and reflection on the word of God, becomes the foundation not only for a growing Christian maturity but also for the priestly state or the state of the counsels to which we have been called.[9] As religious made and continue to make choices, they are drawn into the unity between Father, Son, and Spirit. Every mission, every qualitative calling within the Church, proceeds from the Father, and through the Spirit leads the one called to the Son, who has been called from all eternity by the Father. Religious might ask themselves when did they last prayerfully ponder the beginnings of their own vocation? How far do they still allow this reality that God chose them into their everyday consciousness? Do they consistently understand themselves as involved in God's mission, or do they focus on their ministry? What means might they take to live from this foundation?

6 "The inner life of love is inconceivable without the rhythm of growth, of ever new openness and spontaneity. Love can never give itself sufficiently, can never exhaust its ingenuity in preparing new joys for the beloved, and is never so satisfied with itself and its deeds that it does not look for new proofs of love, is never so familiar with the person of the beloved that it does not crave the wonderment of new knowledge." Ibid., 28.

7 Ibid., 29–30.

8 Ignatius Loyola, *The Spiritual Exercises* 231, trans. George Ganss S.J. (Chicago: Loyola University Press, 1992).

9 There is of course clearly the married state to be emphasized, and Balthasar does so in his work. My focus is on the state of the counsels—religious life and the priestly state, as this is the subject matter of this paper.

Love Expressed in the Paschal Mystery— Ongoing Conversion

The paschal mystery is central to the understanding of our faith. More than this, it is a reality sharply focused for apostolic religious, many of whom have within their constitutions or rule the understanding of a call "to serve beneath the banner of the cross."[10] Indeed, all Christians at some time in their lives must face the full, dramatic horror of the cross when they confront the suffering of Christ for their sinfulness, their alienation from themselves and God through sin, and the continuing suffering of Christ in the contemporary human realities of poverty, violence, and oppression. It is perhaps Paul who best articulates the centrality of the cross, wanting to "know nothing, but Christ crucified" (1 Cor 2:2). This is the supreme "foolishness" of God, which paradoxically reveals God's power and wisdom.[11] This "foolishness" is the ground on which apostolic religious stand. It inevitably means being open and willing to embrace the reality of the cross in their lives both as individuals and as communities. It means living a life of ongoing conversion, and through that way of the cross they are drawn deeply into the life of the Trinity. It inexorably means coming into confrontation with their own very human temptations to independence and self-aggrandizement.

The more deeply human beings allow themselves to be open to the dynamic spirit of God, the more they become aware of themselves in the midst of God's creation, at home in God's world, and invited into God's creative and redemptive work. Credible apostolic ministry in the twenty-first century requires an appreciation and imitation of the self-emptying love that lies at the heart of the Trinity. This is both an invitation and a challenge. The invitation is to a more profound understanding and a deeper participation in the life of the Trinity. The challenge is to personal and communal transformation and pastoral outreach.

10   Cf. Formula of the Institute of the Society of Jesus 1, in *The Constitutions of the Society of Jesus and Their Complementary Norms* (St. Louis, Mo.: Institute of Jesuit Sources, 1996), 3.
11   Cf. 1 Cor 1:18.

Scripture clearly indicates that the reality of the cross can be interpreted only in the context of the Trinity and through faith. Likewise, the full doctrine of the Trinity can be explored only on the basis of a theology of the cross. As Balthasar indicates, the doctrine of the Trinity is "the ever-present, inner presupposition of the Cross."[12] In this "drama" the divine soteriological initiative both invites and initiates human beings into the life of the Trinity. Here, we may glimpse something of the mystery of all mysteries. "God is supremely what he is in giving everything away."[13] It is the Father's primary initiative to give everything in and to the life of the Word. With the self-emptying of the Son there is a further manifestation of the life received from the Father, which continues to be a life realized in self-gift and manifested in the obedience of the Son and the work of the Spirit. The depths of this self-surrender and obedience are fully revealed in the events of the Passion.[14]

Self-Surrender

Self-surrender encapsulates the heart of the vows of poverty and chastity lovingly lived. All authentic being in love, for Lonergan, "is a total self-surrender . . . something in itself, something personal, intimate, and profoundly attuned to the deepest yearnings of the human heart. It constitutes a basic fulfillment of man's being."[15] Many apostolic religious can echo Lonergan's words in the resonance of their own hearts. The very possibility of such self-surrender and the intrinsic nature of this self-surrender to authentically being in love, I would suggest, lies at the heart of the mystery of God and therefore is reflected in human beings created after the image of God. Accordingly, I am suggesting, after the manner of Balthasar, that self-

12 Hans Urs von Balthasar, *Theo-Drama,* vol. 4 (San Francisco: Ignatius Press, 1994), 319.

13 Hans Urs von Balthasar, *Theo-Drama,* vol. 2 (San Francisco: Ignatius Press, 1990), 256.

14 In Von Balthasar's meditation *Heart of the World,* he questions Christ about this obedience: "Do you know what you have chosen, Lord? Are you quite clear about the consequences of your obedience?" (75).

15 Bernard Lonergan, "Theology and Man's Future," in *A Second Collection* (London: Darton, Longman, and Todd, 1974), 145.

surrender is a characteristic of relations within the Trinity and is thus part of the prevenient grace and intimacy that God offers to human beings. Indeed, it is a reflection of God's ongoing love and desire for each person and the consequent blessedness of a human respondent.[16] It is that space of *cor ad cor loquitur,* so important to Saint Ignatius at the heart of the prayer of colloquy. Indeed, Balthasar links this action of self-surrender to the state of Ignatian indifference, and for him the mystery of indifference is "much more a mystery of personal love, and the exchange of wills, one which requires explanation in terms of the Trinity."[17] Is this not the love that the vows call apostolic religious to express?

The act of self-surrender is an act of fruitful love. This is true par excellence in the life, passion, death, and resurrection of Christ, but it is also true in *our* human reality as apostolic religious. Since our lives, however, are obscured by the existence of sin, this act of self-surrender involves an element of risk in a surrender to a God we do not clearly see or perceive. In consequence, true self-surrender always involves some degree of sacrifice or renunciation and a growing desire for real purification. This is a call of ever-deepening love that enables our lives and our service to be truly a Christ light for others. Indeed, the more positive is our response to the divine initiative, the stronger becomes the awareness that even desires, intentions, and motivations need to be surrendered and purified.

This ongoing momentum of self-abandonment in which each level of indifference is sacrificed to an ever deeper self-surrender is clearly illustrated in Balthasar's interpretation of the ministry of Christ. His mission is surrendered in apparent failure, and in Gethsemane it appears that even his capacity to surrender to the Father's will is shaken. The invitation to share in Christ's suffering gives a more profound meaning to self-surrender, because "in the night [of Christ's ag-

16 So Balthasar states in words reminiscent of those of Lonergan above: "In seeking and hearing God, [the human being] experiences the highest joy, that of being fulfilled in itself, but fulfilled in something infinitely greater than itself and, for that very reason, completely fulfilled and made blessed." Hans Urs von Balthasar, *Prayer* (London: SPCK, 1975), 21.

17 Hans Urs von Balthasar, *Therese of Lisieux: The Story of a Mission* (New York: Sheed and Ward, 1963), 239–40.

ony], in which God hid himself, there was the darkness of an extreme love, which could still be affirmed even in non-vision and the naked faith of indifference."[18] So it is that the human act of self-surrender is drawn into the divine act of Trinitarian self-surrender for the salvation of humanity. For Balthasar what takes place in Christ—namely, the divine-human self-surrender—finds its focus and inspiration in what he calls "'God's wound of love' that opening and outpouring of divine life and love in the Trinitarian perichoresis."[19]

Obedience

Obedience may be linked with self-surrender in a way that focuses the dynamic of self-surrender into a moment of attunement to the Ignatian *magis,* urging individuals forward to ever greater holiness. Generous self-surrender may be seen in terms of real commitment to the leading of God's Spirit and the needs of "neighbors" that are central to any concrete mission. Both self-surrender and obedience are crucial to apostolic mission. Without the latter the former runs the risk of being a deceptively self-transcending asceticism.

So self-surrender is a prelude and a prerequisite for the active cooperation of apostolic religious in the divine enterprise. In that self-surrender individuals respond to the invitation to enter into God's creative and redemptive activity. Here obedience is a response of love to that invitation and always includes the divine gift of a greater interior freedom and energy, which in turn assists that response. Thus there develops a deeper intimacy with God through such obedience and a deeper integrity of the human person. Indeed, Balthasar is insistent that obedience is true only when undertaken out of love in a joyful response to the divine initiative of love, not out of fear. It is love alone that prevents obedience from becoming oppressive by engendering life-giving energy and permanence of commitment. In becoming obedient we, as it were, acknowledge for ourselves what is most truly our particular human selfhood, the particular form of

18 Hans Urs von Balthasar, *The Glory of the Lord, V* (Edinburgh: T & T Clark, 1991), 51.
19 Mark A. McIntosh, *Christology from Within* (Notre Dame: University of Notre Dame Press, 2000), 74.

cooperation with God that as individuals we were created to enjoy.[20]

It is clear that the self-surrender of Christ was actualized in obedience, loving and living for others unto death. The pattern of divine love, the cross, must be a pattern of life for apostolic religious who are drawn into the divine trajectory. This is not a destructive burden but rather a source of empowerment enabling a deeper refining of interior dispositions, a more refined *sensus Christi*.

Integrated Apostolic Religious

This emphasis on a gradual refinement of spirit after the manner of Christ is very much in accord with the vision of Ignatius Loyola in the *Spiritual Exercises* that he arranged as a dynamic Christian *Bildung*, a formation of the spirit that is both contemplative and active. The precondition for this formation, the seed ground for the working of the Spirit, is *desire*. What Ignatius seems to be doing by focusing on desire is emphasizing the importance of taking a person exactly where that person is. He stresses a patient waiting with the person, listening and helping the individual slowly uncover the varied clutter that overlays the frail shoots of desire. As desire begins to grow, there is a process of harnessing it to further growth, always with a view to the end, a deeper relationship with God. Therefore, one element of the dynamic is to bring into fruitful and powerful conjunction the obscurely desired and as yet unknown finality and the person's desire for it. The continual process to deepen our relationship with God has its effect: the greater the love, the greater the desire.

The *Spiritual Exercises* were part of Balthasar's own formation as a Jesuit, and they influenced not only the way he prayed but also his developing theological understanding. He did not separate theology and spirituality. He did not see his academic work as separate from the life of prayerful contemplation and activity in the community of the Church. He insisted that one could do theology properly only "on one's knees." For contemporary apostolic religious the question needs to be posed, how far do we separate prayer from work? Is

---

20 See also Mark McIntosh's discussion of obedience in *Christology from Within,* 75–87.

there a key integration such that all our apostolates are undertaken metaphorically "on our knees"? Is there still such integration in the times of real difficulty when the cross is more apparent in large ways or even in the small irritating matters of everyday encounters with others? In the drama of our lives are we aware of the divine and human dimensions—the ongoingly intersubjective character of the divine encounter with human beings?[21] There are two essential dimensions to the drama, the human and the divine, but these are not in competition. The divine freedom expressed in the persons of the Trinity both constitutes the reality of human freedom and preserves its distinctive character in the interrelationship with the divine.

For Ignatius, contemplation and action are intertwined. It is not a form of contemplation that leads to epistemological issues, our activity of gaining knowledge. Rather, it is a contemplation that brings one to an action that leads to the discovery of truth. Such a discovery is consequent upon participation in a world we come to know in its beauty and truth through the self-giving love of God. We can reflect on the truth of Christian revelation only by becoming a player in the midst of this world, involved as we are in the passion and the Passion of God.[22]

Ignatius always endeavors to preserve a spirit of openness, which is the only true response to a God who is ever greater. At the heart of Ignatius's work there is a tension between intimacy and distance, likeness and unlikeness, profound love and the "fear of the Lord which is the beginning of wisdom," rooted in reverence and awe. Balthasar and Ignatius are at one in their attempt to articulate the reality of God, who is always greater than any conception of him, God of ever-

21 For a more detailed exploration of von Balthasar's theodramatics, see particularly, Ben Quash, "Drama and the Ends of Modernity," in *Balthasar At The End of Modernity*, ed. Lucy Gardner, David Moss, Ben Quash, and Graham Ward, 139–71 (Edinburgh: T & T Clark, 1999). Also Ben Quash, "The Theo-Drama" in *The Cambridge Companion to Hans Urs von Balthasar*, ed. Edward T. Oakes and David Moss, 143–57 (Cambridge: Cambridge University Press, 2004).

22 "The life common to Christ and the Church is . . . actual life poised between perdition and redemption, sinfulness and sanctity. The existence of sin within the field of force of grace, the impact, here and now, between despairing obduracy and crucified love, these, and not a colourless and static world of philosophy, are the matter of theology. This is why it cannot be expressed solely in the sleek and passionless form of the treatise, but demands movement, sharp debate. . . . The virile language of deep and powerful emo-

greater dissimilarity.[23] It is through this reality of God, this dialectic of seeming presence and absence, that God entices us forward and deeper into the divine mystery present in all our contemplation and action. The reality of this dialectic also gives rise to a divine dynamism at the heart of creation, a dynamism that is always new in each historical circumstance.[24]

Love Manifested in Ecclesial Commitment

For Balthasar, as for Ignatius, the primary embodiment of this work of reconciliation in contemporary times lies in the Church. For both men the institutional structure of the Church was important. Ignatius expressed his understanding of a true relationship with the Church in his "Rules for Thinking, Judging and Feeling with the Church."[25] Here, it is clear that Ignatius could see no definitive conflict between the freedom of the individual conscience and the teaching of the institutional Church.[26] These men were committed to a similar understanding. Within the life and work of both Ignatius and Balthasar it is clear that they are not attempting, in their commitment to the institutional Church, to usurp the dynamic action of the Holy Spirit, calling individuals to ever greater holiness and the fullness of the life of grace. Rather, they seemed to be able to hold these two realities in a creative tension that was fruitful for the life of the Church and the lives of those whom they influenced.

For Balthasar, his understanding of Ignatius's "Rules" led him to emphasize the Marian character of the Church, which he linked to the graced openness and receptivity of Mary and which he saw as

---

tion." Hans Urs von Balthasar, *Explorations in Theology I: The Word Made Flesh* (San Francisco: Ignatius Press, 1989), 204–5.

23 *Maior dissimilitude,* classically defined by the Fourth Lateran Council 1215.

24 Ben Quash, "Ignatian Dramatics," *The Way* 38 (January 1988): 77–86.

25 This is the term utilized by George Ganss, S.J., in his translation and commentary on *The Spiritual Exercises,* 133. Earlier authorities used the term "Rules for Thinking with the Church."

26 Ben Quash makes a similar point when he states, "Ignatius was committed to the view that there could be no absolute conflict between the nearness of the God of his conscience and experience [the grace from within] and the institutional direction of the official Church [the God from without]." "Ignatian Dramatics," 85.

the disposition of commitment to the Church. He saw the primary issue in Ignatius's rules as focusing on an understanding of "obedient readiness." "Ignatius does not speak of 'love for the Church' but of readiness before her, evidently in order to be drawn into her love for Christ, and through Christ for all human beings."[27] Balthasar is also insistent that alongside the Marian character of the Church there is also a Petrine character and that together these constitute the inner dimensions of the Church founded by Christ. Mary's full and free "yes" to the will of God is expressed in a certain integrity of person and life. "We can say that she represents the perfect example of the existential priesthood, namely the perfect correspondence between person and office, where all is ordered to the divine mission."[28] It is the figure of Saint John, the beloved disciple, the friend whom Jesus loved and who was so close to him at the last supper, who represents for Balthasar the religious life. Along with Mary, Saint John represents the Church of love, which is brought to full expression in the faithful living of the evangelical counsels. Apostolic religious make a singular contribution to this reality. In understanding the reality of the Church, then, Balthasar calls us to see Mary, John, and Peter in relationship and proposes the Gospel scene of one of the resurrection appearances for our consideration. Receiving the news from Mary Magdalene, John and Peter both run to the empty tomb. Although John—symbolizing the Church of love—arrives first, he gives precedence to Peter, who symbolizes the Church of office. It is clear from this representation that Balthasar does not balk at the Church of love making submission to the institutional Church. But at the same time he draws our attention also to the reality that the institutional Church has no other function than to serve the Church of love.[29]

In the contemporary Church we are challenged to live this ten-

27 Hans Urs von Balthasar, "Die Kirche lieben?" *Pneuma und Institution,* 162–200, cited in Werner Loser S.J., "The Ignatian Exercises in the Work of Hans Urs Von Balthasar," in *Hans Urs von Balthasar His Life and Work,* ed. David Schindler, 103–20 (San Francisco: Ignatius Press, 1991).

28 John O'Donnell, S.J., *Hans Urs von Balthasar* (London: Geoffrey Chapman, 1992), 133. I am indebted to the late Fr. John O'Donnell—who first taught me theology at Heythrop College, University of London—for conversations 2000–2001 around these points.

29 "For Balthasar, office in the Church is meant to be the crystallization of love." Ibid.

sion in ways that are equally life-giving. It is clear from what has already been indicated that the possibility of living in such an ecclesial way so that the mission of Christ may be promoted involves a deeper contemplative living that finds expression in an active apostolate. Central to a living out of this ecclesial relationship is as I have indicated elsewhere,[30] a hermeneutical principle that benignly interprets the words or actions of another. This is a valid hermeneutical stance, drawing its authority from the *Spiritual Exercises* of Ignatius.[31] It is also a stance that arises from and contributes to a deep contemplative disposition, enabling this to be the foundation from which action arises within the mission.

The contemporary Church, because she lives in the reality of these tensions, "lives in an incomprehensible place between earth and heaven, between death and eternal life, between the old world that is passing away and the new and incorruptible world."[32] In this liminal space, the Church is poised to respond both to her Lord and to the world within which she has temporal existence.[33] The heart of the Church is the celebration of the Eucharist. The Eucharist is at the center of life for an apostolic religious. It is here in the gift of the Eucharist that the mystery of the Church's role is revealed, for the Eucharist is "a reciprocal communion between Christ and the Church and ultimately between the Trinity and the entire cosmos."[34] Here, the Trinitarian life of God is manifested and so also "the ultimate nature of created being in their difference and unity."[35] So also is revealed within the Eucharist the end to which the Church is ori-

30   Gill Goulding, I.B.V.M., *Creative Perseverance* (Ottawa Novalis, 2003), 143.

31   See the Presupposition of the Spiritual Exercises.

32   Hans Urs von Balthasar, *Explorations in Theology II* (San Francisco: Ignatius Press, 1991), 511.

33   Cf. *Lumen Gentium* (Dogmatic Constitution on the Church) #9; *Gaudium et Spes* (Pastoral Constitution on the Modern World) #41, where it states that the Church defines itself as "an instrument for the redemption of all, sent forth into the whole world as the light of the world and the salt of the earth." But also Church defines itself as the "sacrament by which Christ's mission is extended to include the whole of man, body and soul, and through that totality the whole of nature created by God."

34   Nicholas Healy and David Schindler, "For the Life of the World: Hans Urs von Balthasar on the Church as Eucharist," in *The Cambridge Companion to Hans Urs von Balthasar* (Cambridge: University of Cambridge Press, 2006), 51–63.

35   Ibid.

ented, "for the goal of the entire ecclesial reality is the salvation and rescuing of the world."[36] In the Pauline formula all things are to be reconciled in Christ. Indeed, Healy and Schindler argue that this inclusion in Christ of all creation means also that "creation is taken into the mission of Christ to the extent that it shares in his mission of mediating the Trinitarian love of Father, Son and Spirit by realizing its original purpose in being created."[37] In a depiction reminiscent of the Ignatian *Contemplatio* (the Contemplation to Attain the Love of God), Balthasar indicates that in the Trinity's plan for the world, creation was a gift from the Father to the Son revelatory of the life of the Trinity. And in the redemptive work of Christ there is a return of this gift of creation from the Son to the Father. Human beings are drawn into this divine dynamic at the heart of creation.[38] In the *Contemplatio* Ignatius encourages the one making the *Spiritual Exercises* to become aware of the gifted nature of all reality, and to respond by a prayer of self-donation, an offering of gift of self, in response to the gift of Self that God gives in creation and supremely in Christ.

This is a life-giving exchange of gifts, and this understanding lies at the heart of the reality of Eucharist. It is "the event whereby Christ communicates the whole of his human and Trinitarian life by gathering into himself the whole of creation; and the event whereby the Church offers herself and ultimately the whole cosmos by receiving the gift of Christ and entering into his mission to renew the cosmos."[39]

If there is an intended Eucharistic destiny at the heart of creation,

---

36   Balthasar, *Explorations in Theology II*, 316.

37   "For the Life of the World," 54.

38   "The world can be thought of as the gift of the Father [who is both Begetter and Creator] to the Son, since the Father wishes to sum up all things in heaven and earth in the Son, as head [Eph 1:10]; thus the Son takes this gift—just as he takes the gift of Godhead—as an opportunity to thank and glorify the Father." *Theo-Drama*, 2:262.

39   Healy and Schindler, "For the Life of the World," 57. Cf. There is one incident of graced awareness in the life of Ignatius that seems to bear a remarkable resemblance to this architectonic vision. This understanding appears to the author to be reminiscent of what one senses in the graced understanding granted to Ignatius beside the river Cardoner, where "the eyes of his understanding began to open. He beheld no vision, but he saw and understood many things, spiritual as well as those concerning faith and learning. . . . He received a great illumination in his understanding." Autobiography #30, in *Saint Ignatius of Loyola: Personal Writings*, trans. with introduction and notes by Joseph Munitiz, S.J., and Philip Endean, S.J. (London: Penguin Classics, 1996).

then an abiding openness to the world is a primordial stance for the Church and especially for apostolic religious. Balthasar emphasizes through his work that the vocation of the Church is "to pour itself out for the life of the world, even as the world finds herself in the life of the Eucharist."[40] The Church will be enabled to do so the more deeply rooted its members are in the life of the Trinity. This will involve for religious their entry into the way of self-gift, self-surrender, and obedience, for it is the way of the Persons of the Trinity.

Relationship between Religious Life and Priesthood

In Balthasar's theology religious life and the life of priesthood are closely linked. This is an insight that we might fruitfully ponder. With regard to the priesthood Christ continues to be present in the world through his word, his sacraments, and the ministerial priesthood. Since no human being is able to adequately represent Christ, Christ as it were lays hold of a man and through the sacrament of holy orders enables that man to represent him. No human being is fully able to do this, and, therefore, there is always a real gap between the priest and the office to which he has been called. The subjective holiness of the priest never matches the objective representation of his office. This gives the potential for great humility, but regardless Christ guarantees that when the priest acts in his name by preaching his word and celebrating his sacraments he is present to the faithful with his grace through the action of the priest. Theologian John O'Donnell has written, "If the evangelical counsels represent primarily the subjective surrender of the consecrated person to Christ, the priesthood emphasizes his objective office in the community."[41] It is important that religious life and the priesthood are seen as complementary and vital for the life of the Church, not as competitive or alternative vocations.[42] In the tradition of the

40 "For the Life of the World," 63.
41 O'Donnell, *Hans Urs von Balthasar,* 132.
42 "On the one hand, the subjective surrender of the religious to Christ becomes objective as he or she is inserted into a religious family with a rule approved by the Church. On the other hand, the objective ministry of the priest calls for a way of life in conformity with the ministry, a way of life that makes the ministry credible."

Church there is a clear recognition of an inner coherence between these two vocations.

Conclusion: The Language of Love

How are we to speak of the treasure of apostolic religious life to-day? What is the vocabulary of the love that drives us? The publication of the decrees of the 35th General Congregation of the Society of Jesus might help us, for it evoked surprise amongst some readers.[43] The sections dealing with the Society's identity and charism, the relationship with the Holy Father, and the decree on obedience generated the most interest. The surprise element is the language in which these decrees are written. There is a certain expectation that Jesuit decrees will be analytical, precise, and action oriented. These particular sections use the language of the affect, not merely the emotions but involving the deepest place of the spirit, and call for an engagement of the heart of the reader. They use words such as "fervor" and "zeal" and "fidelity," words that were prevalent in the vocabulary of the founders and foundresses of many orders of apostolic religious. They call for a contemplative reading, a prayerful pondering, and they evoke great consolation. They recall Jesuits and members of the Ignatian family to their roots, just as the conciliar Fathers at Vatican II requested. It is imperative that we reclaim something of this contemplative way of proceeding with regard to our prayer, our planning, and our practices as apostolic religious.[44] Certainly if we do so as both individuals and communities, it will make a difference and assist the transformation of our institutes. In such a case, the faithful loving life of even one member has enormous influence. Graced joyful fidelity bears witness to the faithfulness of our Triune God; it is divine love flowing in us and through all our apostolic efforts that gives real credibility.

43 I am indebted for these ideas to conversation with Fr. Peter Bisson, S.J., a delegate to GC 35 from the Province of English Speaking Canada and a member of the preparatory commission for the General Congregation.

44 In an e-mail correspondence with Sr. Sara Butler, the possibility of something akin to the Institute of Priestly Formation but for apostolic religious was raised. Certainly ways of helping to form religious in this way could be very fruitful.

Seven

Apostolic Religious Life in the Post–Vatican II Church

Ongoing Challenges of Renewal—
Perfect and Imperfect Love

KURT PRITZL, O.P.

Perfect charity or complete love, the divine reality signified by the opening words of the Decree on the Appropriate Renewal of the Religious Life of the Second Vatican Council (*Perfectae Caritatis*), provides the theme of this essay.[1] This theme is pursued insofar as love, as it ranges in human life from earthly mortal love to charity, constitutes the practical basis and effective engine for meeting ongoing challenges of renewal of apostolic religious life. The Council's

---

1   The Decree on the Appropriate Renewal of the Religious Life, referred to hereafter by its Latin title, *Perfectae Caritatis*, and cited as *PC,* was promulgated on October 28, 1965. All documents of the Second Vatican Council are cited and quoted from Walter M. Abbott, S.J., general editor, *The Documents of Vatican II: All Sixteen Official Texts Promulgated by the Ecumenical Council 1963–1965 Translated from the Latin,* intro. Lawrence Cardinal Shehan, translations directed by Joseph Gallagher (London: Geoffrey Chapman, 1966), by section and page number.

Dogmatic Constitution on the Church (*Lumen Gentium*) had earlier forcefully made the point that charity, "the first and most necessary gift,"[2] is the ultimate guide and engine of holiness for all the faithful, and in a special way for religious: "For charity, as the bond of perfection and the fulfillment of the law (cf. Col 3:14; Rom 13:10), rules over all the means of attaining holiness, gives life to them, and makes them work. Hence it is the love of God and of neighbor which points out the true disciple of Christ."[3] After more than thirty years of momentous and unexpected change in the world, the Church, and religious life since the Council, Pope John Paul II's post-synodal apostolic exhortation *Vita Consecrata* emphasized the same principle, writing of "the grace of this special communion of love with Christ" and "this special grace of intimacy which, in the consecrated life, makes possible and even demands the total gift of self in the profession of the evangelical counsels."[4] One instance of the dynamic of charity at work in the founding of a religious order is given in the acts of canonization of Saint Dominic:

> Frequently he made a special personal petition that God would deign to grant him a genuine charity, effective in caring for and obtaining

2   Dogmatic Constitution on the Church, §42 (p. 70); hereafter referred to by its Latin title, *Lumen Gentium*, and cited as *LG*. This decree was promulgated November 21, 1964.

3   *LG* §42 (71). This quotation regards the universal call to holiness; specific reference to the fundamental role of the perfection of charity in consecrated life is abundantly given in chapter 6 of the decree, where §44 (74) gives one early instance: "The faithful of Christ can bind themselves to the three previously mentioned counsels either by vows, or by other sacred bonds which are like vows in their purpose. Through such a bond a person is totally dedicated to God by an act of supreme love, and is committed to the honor and service of God under a new and special title." See further in §44 (74–75) and at §45 (76): "For by that practice [of the evangelical counsels] is uniquely fostered the perfection of love for God and neighbor." See also §46 (77).

4   *Post-Synodal Apostolic Exhortation "Vita Consecrata" of the Holy Father John Paul II to the Bishops and Clergy, Religious Orders and Congregations, Societies of Apostolic Life, Secular Institutes, and all the Faithful on the Consecrated Life and Its Mission in the Church and in the World* (Vatican City: Vatican Press, 1996), §§15–16 (24), promulgated on March 25, 1996. All citations and quotations are from this volume by section and page number, hereafter cited as *VC*. See also *VC* §42 (72): "Love led Christ to the gift of self, even to the supreme sacrifice of the Cross. So too, among this disciples, *there can be no true unity without that unconditional mutual love* which demands a readiness to serve others generously, a willingness to welcome them as they are, without 'judging' them (cf. *Mt* 7:1–2), and an ability to forgive up to 'seventy times seven' (*Mt* 18:22)" (emphasis in the text).

the salvation of men. For he believed that only then would he be truly a member of Christ, when he had given himself totally for the salvation of men, just as the Lord Jesus, the Savior of all, had offered himself completely for our salvation. So, for this work, after a lengthy period of careful and provident planning, he founded the Order of Friars Preachers.[5]

This essay discusses the complex reality of love, active and engaged concretely in real life, as the necessary condition for genuine and meaningful ongoing renewal of consecrated life, with respect either to the perennial and constant need for renewal or to the specific needs for renewal today.[6] The point may seem obvious, and it is, but the theme is worth exploration, if only because for all its obviousness, renewal in religious life has been neither automatic nor easy.

Ongoing challenges of renewal of apostolic religious life in the post–Vatican II Church is a large topic. The Church is universal, and there is great diversity in religious life. Thus, there are limits and parameters to my reflections, including the following. (1) To the extent to which this essay speaks to the contemporary and specific need for renewal, in contradistinction to the constant need for renewal in even the best of religious life, I address the scene in the developed rather than the developing world. (2) This essay pursues an analysis that more likely fits more established religious communities, rather than newer ones still in the joy and fervor of their youth. (3) As the reference to Saint Dominic indicates, my experience and observations of religious life, which ground these reflections and which are, I hope, adequate for saying something useful, are nevertheless perforce limited. (4) *Perfectae Caritatis* from the Second Vatican Council and the apostolic exhortation *Vita Consecrata* some thirty years later are the bounding documents for this paper. Both

5   Quoted from the Office of Readings for August 8 in *The Liturgy of the Hours according to the Roman Rite,* vol. 4: *Ordinary Time, Weeks 18–34* (New York: Catholic Book Publishing, 1975), 1302.

6   On the need for constant renewal within religious life, see *VC* §109 (196): "You know well that you have set out on a journey of continual conversion, of exclusive dedication to the love of God and of your brothers and sisters, in order to bear ever more splendid witness to the grace which transfigures Christian life." See also §110 (198) on "day by day" renewal in Christ.

provide general principles for renewal with some indications of the contemporary situation in their respective times, with much about specific conditions left as a subtext, especially in *Perfectae Caritatis.*[7] Much has changed, of course, in the world, in the Church, and in religious life, since the Second Vatican Council called for renewal of consecrated life. These momentous changes, which do surface in *Vita Consecrata,* have continued if not accelerated since the dawn of the new millennium.[8] Details of the current situation and the pressing challenges and opportunities of our times have been richly addressed in other essays in this volume and are not my immediate concern. I offer as a complement, and one with sufficient specificity, I hope, an analysis offering a formula for ongoing renewal based on practical aspects of the forms of love relevant to religious life. Love has a fundamental practical character with concrete applications to contemporary religious life in relation to contemporary society and culture.

The analysis in this essay depends on a basic philosophical distinction with respect to the workings of human character and the ultimate motivations and springs of human action. This distinction

---

7 Cf. *PC* §1 (467–68) with *VC* §2 (4), §4 (7), and §13 (19).

8 For example, *VC* makes explicit reference to difficulties facing religious life since the Council (§2 [4–5]; §3 [6]; §13 [18]; makes more explicit reference to technocratic, utilitarian, individualistic, secularistic, and relativistic cultural conditions that seem to have accelerated since the 1960s (§43 [74]; §67 [121]; §85 [156]; §§87–92 [159–67]; §103 [187]; §104 [190]); notes the emergence of new religious orders and ecclesial communities, the work done to rewrite constitutions and other foundational documents by religious institutes, and the formation of federations and unions of religious communities (§56 [96]; §62 [109]); considers the role of feminism in the Church and society (§58 [99]); and emphasizes the need for fidelity to the magisterium (§46 [79]; §47 [80–81]). For an example of one very specific issue, the wearing of religious habits, *PC* §17 (478) calls for one form of renewal, stating that "religious habits should be simple and modest, at once poor and becoming. They should meet the requirements of health and be suited to the circumstances of the time and place as well as to the services required by those who wear them." It goes on to mandate that "habits of men and women which do not correspond to those norms are to be changed" *VC* §25 (41). The effects of change are obvious in a call for another form of renewal: "Since the habit is a sign of consecration, poverty, and membership in a particular Religious family, I join the Fathers of the Synod in strongly recommending to men and women religious that they wear their proper habit, suitably adapted to conditions of time and place. Where valid reasons of their apostolate call for it, Religious, in conformity with the norms of their Institute, may also dress in a simple and modest manner, with an appropriate symbol, in such a way that their consecration is recognizable" (ibid.).

takes some form as this—the distinction between love and hate, attraction and aversion, desire and fear, pleasure and pain.[9] Humans act either to attain what they love or long for, on the one hand, or to avoid what they hate or fear, on the other. In a concrete case of action the situation is often mixed, but one of love or hate predominates, and explicitly or implicitly every philosophical outlook gives ultimate priority to one over the other. For example, the classical tradition of Plato, Aristotle, and Aquinas gives priority to love or desire, whereas Hobbes in early modernity and Nietzsche in late modernity acknowledge as the natural condition of human life the war of each against all. Plato in the *Phaedo* has Socrates note that in actual life the two sides of the distinction are found together and have their interplay in how we determine to act:

> Socrates sat up on the bed, bent his leg and rubbed it with his hand, and as he rubbed he said: "What a strange thing that which men call pleasure seems to be, and how astonishing the relation it has with what is thought to be its opposite, namely pain! A man cannot have both at the same time. Yet if he pursues and catches the one, he is almost always bound to catch the other also, like two creatures with one head. I think that if Aesop had noted this he would have composed a fable that a god wishes to reconcile their opposition but could not do so, so he joined their two heads together, and therefore when a man has the one, the other follows later. This seems to be happening to me. My bonds caused me pain in my leg, and now pleasure seems to be following."[10]

The good philosophical answer, in my judgment, is that love predominates in the natural mix of human life.[11] The Christian answer

9   These are not synonymous pairings, but they are close enough in meaning to serve the present analysis.

10   *Phaedo* 60b1–c7, quoted from the translation of G. M. A. Grube in Plato, *Complete Works,* ed. with introduction and notes by John M. Cooper (Indianapolis: Hackett Publishing, 1997), 52.

11   This basic point holds notwithstanding the further issue of properly directed love or longing. This further, fundamental issue is well covered in our documents, which are very articulate about the guides, norms, and measures of properly directed love. *PC* §2 (468), e.g., includes as principles for appropriate renewal (a) the Gospel as the fundamental norm and "supreme law" and (b) the specific charisms of individual communities. The

goes farther, namely, to the supernatural reality of the pure Love which is God without any trace of its opposite, without need, want, or lack, found in the life of the Trinity, and in which we share in faith by grace through the saving death of Christ.[12] Pope John Paul II's admonition "Be not afraid!" repeated from the beginnings of his pontificate, has its ultimate warrant in the reality of divine love without opposite, which is present by grace in Christian life, despite the contending forces of love and hate, desire and aversion, that condition the earthly life of individuals, communities, and the world as a whole. The consecrated life based on the profession of the evangelical counsels is to be a unique, distinctive, and outstanding sign not only of the ultimacy and triumph of love over hate, strife, and fear, but of the supernatural love possessed and lived now, which transcends the natural interplay of love and hate, of longing and fear, in human life. Thus, disciples are called to love even their enemies and to forgive endlessly, doing it all joyfully and willingly in freedom. Thus, those who have professed the evangelical counsels are called to a renunciation of the world and to a life without earthly cares, realizing for the whole Church the life of heavenly realities that is already in this world.[13]

This is much to hope for, but it is what Christ offers in a particularly urgent and compelling way in the call to religious life, and what he makes possible when the call is accepted. The constant need for conversion and renewal in such a life, however, becomes quite clear. If these philosophical and theological points about love and hate in relation to action are granted, love, not its opposite, is the ultimate and only unfailing force for authentic and genuine renewal in religious life, as in any life. One pressing issue for ongoing renewal today, then, is to bring such general considerations, valid as I find them, to concrete, particular, and sustained application. Grace

---

revision of constitutions and other foundational documents required by the Council has sharpened and focused these documents as guides and measures of religious life (PC §3 [469]). There is no lack of solid and inspirational direction for rightly directed love and desire in religious life.

12   VC §§17–22 (26–36) emphasizes in a beautiful way the Trinitarian life of love and community as it relates to consecrated life.

13   VC §§26–27 (42–5) emphasizes the eschatological dimensions of consecrated life.

perfects nature, and God's grace works in the details of our lives—both the specific conditions and circumstances of life in our various religious families and the specific conditions and circumstances of our larger culture and society.

Lumen Gentium affirms that the "religious state reveals in a unique way that the kingdom of God and its overmastering necessities are superior to all earthly considerations. Finally, to all men it shows wonderfully at work within the Church the surpassing greatness of the force of Christ the King and the boundless power of the Holy Spirit."[14] This is, to my mind, one of the most compelling features of religious life, that people can actually live happily in the service of God and others, giving up the goods of marriage, possessions, and free decision making—that the grace and love of God at work in authentic religious life is real enough to give one's whole life to it.[15] *Perfectae Caritatis* adds that a "life consecrated by the profession of the counsels is of surpassing value" and that "[s]uch a life has a necessary role to play in the circumstances of the present age."[16]

Despite the beauty of this transcendent or other-worldly way of life lived now in the world and its necessity for the world today, *Vita Consecrata* finds it necessary, nonetheless, to cite decreasing numbers of vocations and the disappearance of some religious institutes, including the possibility of dioceses without the presence of members of religious communities at all. The document adds, however, the proper perspective in the face of these losses: "The various difficulties stemming from the decline in personnel and apostolates *must in no way lead to a loss of confidence in the evangelical vitality of the consecrated life* [emphasis Pritzl], which will always be present and active in the Church. While individual Institutes have no claim to permanence, the consecrated life will continue to sustain among the faithful the response of love towards God and neighbor."[17] It

14   *LG* §44 (75).

15   This life lived "for God alone not only by dying to sin (cf. Rom. 6:11) but also by renouncing the world" is what *PC* §5 (470) calls "an ampler manifestation" of baptismal consecration.

16   *PC* §1 (467).

17   *VC* §63 (112–13; emphasis in the text); §48 (84); see also *VC* §105 (191): "'What would become of the world if there were no Religious'? Beyond all superficial assessments

also states that "the consecrated life is destined to remain a shining witness to the inseparable love of God and love of neighbour," but then immediately argues that "what must be avoided at all costs is the actual breakdown of consecrated life, a collapse which is not measured by a decrease in numbers but by a failure to cling steadfastly to the Lord and to personal vocation and mission."[18]

The ultimate imperative of renewal, as John Paul II states, is fidelity to the mission of love by professed religious, rather than numbers. A momentous and sad change in the Church of the developed world since the Second Vatican Council, however, is the prospect of religious life becoming a token or quaint presence in the normal life of the Church by virtue of low numbers relative to the overall population of the faithful.[19] The ongoing challenge of renewal of religious life today includes this dimension. In arguing for an effective and practical engagement with love as a basis for ongoing renewal in religious life, for the sake of both greater fidelity among professed religious and an increase in vocations, I want to argue in a way that specifically addresses the threat of tokenism and quaintness by an analysis that indicates more rather than less engagement and connection with what I have just called here "the normal life of the church as a whole."[20] By this phrase I want to designate the life

---

of its usefulness, the consecrated life is important precisely in its being *unbounded generosity and love,* and this all the more so in a world that risks being suffocated in the whirlpool of the ephemeral" (emphasis in the text). *L'Osservatore Romano* reported on February 4, 2008, that the overall number of men and women religious in the church worldwide was 945,210, down by 94,790 from one year before.

18   *VC* §63 (113–14).

19   This is true even in the United States, which, compared to the pervasive secularism of Western Europe, is relatively religious in outlook and practice.

20   The pressing demands for contemporary renewal of religious life, whose fruit, it is trusted, would include an increase of vocations, include this issue of biodiversity within the Church. Religious communities cannot become like the ivory-billed woodpecker in Alabama (also known as the "Lord God Bird" for the reaction seeing one evoked, because of its size and beauty), possibly glimpsed from time to time. The argument that follows depends on this biodiversity, where the different ways of life in the Church support one another, as *VC* §31 (52) points out: "The vocations to the lay life, to the ordained ministry and to the consecrated life can be considered paradigmatic, inasmuch as all particular vocations, considered separately or as a whole, lead back to them, in accordance with the richness of God's gift. These vocations are also at service to one another, for the growth of the Body of Christ in history and for its mission in the world."

of the lay faithful and the life of marriage and raising of children.

This essay's attempt to spell out this engagement and connection capitalizes (1) on the bonds that exist between all the faithful for mutual support because of the universal call to holiness and (2) on the truth of two interconnected paradoxes of religious life that figure in religious life precisely because of its renunciation of the world and its special dedication to living more exclusively by spiritual means.[21]

The first paradox of religious life to address can be formulated with the help of a principle first articulated by Plato, namely, that corruption of the best is the worst.[22] This is not to assert that consecrated life is a better life than other lives in the Church, but to affirm the special and distinctive character of consecrated life as a complete dedication to God's service in answer to God's specific call.[23] Religious life entails living the evangelical counsels in a radical way, including forsaking the intimacy of marriage, parenting, ownership of goods, freedom to do as one pleases, and so on. Religious life, even in its most active forms, requires a privacy and quiet for prayer and contemplation that is not normal in married and family life. It also provides a freedom for worship of God and service that is not otherwise possible.

Full and authentic religious life is possible only by dependence on God's grace and by a divine love of the life—love of the evangelical counsels, of the rule and constitutions, of the practices and way

---

21   *LG* §40 (66–67) on the universal call to holiness in loving service to each other states:

> The Lord Jesus, the divine Teacher and Model of all perfection, preached holiness of life to each and every one of His disciples, regardless of their situation: "You therefore are to be perfect, even as your heavenly Father is perfect" (Mt. 5:48). He Himself stands as the Author and Finisher of the holiness of life. For he sent the Holy Spirit upon all men that He might inspire them from within to love God with their whole heart and their whole soul, with all their mind and all their strength (cf. Mk. 12:30) and that they might love one another as Christ loved them (cf. Jn. 13.34; 15: 12). . . . Thus it is evident to everyone that all the faithful of Christ of whatever rank or status are called to the fullness of the Christian life and to the perfection of charity. By this holiness a more human way of life is promoted even in this earthly society.

22   See, e.g., *Republic* 2.380e3–381c10.

23   The Platonic principle is used in its original form since the corresponding notion, that the corruption of the special and the distinctive is special and distinctive, while true, does not capture the point.

of life, and of one's brothers and sisters in the life. It is said of Saint Dominic repeatedly in the acts of canonization that he loved poverty.[24] Such an observation is appropriate to acts of canonization, for love of poverty, the active desire for and wanting of poverty, is a sign of sanctity. Already in the early Dominican community there were tendencies to eat delicacies, ride horses, acquire rich vestments, accept properties, and expand small cells, all of which Saint Dominic attempted to prevent.[25] *Perfectae Caritatis* specifies the process of "a continuous return . . . to the original inspiration behind a given community" and endorses the principle that "loyal recognition and safekeeping . . . be accorded to the spirit of founders" for appropriate renewal to take place.[26] This process and this principle for renewal are not just for the sake of recalling ideals, as important as that is, but for rekindling the love that animated the original community through its founder, something that tends to dissipate with time and growth in numbers.

Along with a natural tendency to laxness, apart from much strength of grace, is the fact that the essential conditions of consecrated life, conditions that make for freedom to worship God, to study, and to serve others, are materially such by their nature that they can be too readily enjoyed for their own sake. While life may

24 "He loved poverty very much, and zealously incited the brethren to have a similar love. Asked how he [Brother John of Spain] knew this, he answered that Brother Dominic gloried in the poorest clothing, and that, having given up all temporal things, he often exhorted the brethren to love poverty, and this is the presence of the witness." *Saint Dominic: Biographical Documents,* ed. with introduction by Francis C. Lehner, O.P. (Washington, D.C.: Thomist Press, 1964), 117; see also 110; 116; 120–21; 126; 129–30; 134; and 140.

25 Ibid., 110, 118, 120, 126, and 143.

26 *PC* §2 (468). *VC* §93 (167–68) beautifully connects the perfection of charity to saintly founders in a passage worth quoting at length:

> One of the concerns frequently expressed at the Synod was that the consecrated life should be nourished *from the wellspring of a sound and deep spirituality.* This is a primary requirement, inscribed in the very essence of the consecrated life by the fact that, just as every baptized person, and indeed even more so, those who profess the evangelical counsels must aspire with all their strength to the perfection of charity. This commitment is clearly evidenced in the many examples of holy founders and foundresses, and of so many consecrated persons who have borne faithful witness to Christ to the point of martyrdom. To tend toward holiness: this is in summary the programme of every consecrated life, particularly in the perspective of its renewal on the threshold of the Third Millennium. [emphasis in the text]

be simple, there can be a level of economic security in religious life, along with a sense of entitlement, that is missing even from middle-class life among the lay faithful. There is privacy and possible detachment from others in community not normal in lay family life, including relative independence from others, even superiors, beyond anything a spouse may seek. The freedom to serve all and any others that comes from celibate chastity can be prone to the "problem of socialism," namely, to belong to everyone is to belong to no one. *Lumen Gentium* says that the devotion of the professed religious is "to the welfare of the whole Church,"[27] but this devotion must be lived out concretely. Examples could be multiplied. The general point is that the structures, practices, and circumstances of religious life, including ones that are absolutely essential to it and necessary for the spiritual life and pursuit of holiness to which profession of the evangelical counsels is dedicated, can be readily degraded if not corrupted when not practiced in the spirit of divine love under the influence of grace. Even minor corruption of the best injures religious life. It can also indeed be the worst, as the scandals of the recent past have shown.

This is the paradox. On the one hand, the solid and essential practices of "religious families give their members the support of greater stability in their way of life, a proven method of acquiring perfection, fraternal association in the militia of Christ, and liberty strengthened by obedience," as *Lumen Gentium* points out, concluding: "Thus these religious can securely fulfill and faithfully observe their religious profession, and rejoicing in spirit make progress on the road of charity."[28] On the other hand, the practices and routines of religious life can provide structures encouraging superficial observance, lack of authenticity, limited engagement in ministry, and distance from others. The means of grace specific for religious life are the primary basis for growth in holiness and the principal means of conversion and renewal, and yet life within these structures and practices, when external or lax, can work the opposite. The counter-

27 LG §44 (75); cf. PC §12 (474) regarding the chastity of religious life: "For it liberates the human heart in a unique way (cf. 1 Cor. 7:32–35) and causes it to burn with greater love for God and all mankind."
28 LG §43 (73–74).

productive possibilities and tendencies, risked by daring to attempt religious life, which this paradox indicates, needs remedy.

The second paradox about religious life that requires consideration is its relation to marriage. The material meaning and signification of marriage is found in actual marriage of men and women. In distinguishing consecrated life, *Lumen Gentium* states that consecrated life is a "better symbol" of the marriage of Christ to the Church:

> It is true that through baptism he has died to sin and has been consecrated to God. However, in order to derive more abundant fruit from this baptismal grace, he intends, by the profession of the evangelical counsels in the Church, to free himself from those obstacles which might draw him away from the fervor of charity and the perfection of divine worship. Thus he is more intimately consecrated to divine service. This consecration gains in perfection since by virtue of firmer and steadier bonds it serves as a better symbol of the unbreakable link between Christ and his Spouse, the Church.[29]

Perfectae Caritatis reaffirms this idea particularly with respect to celibate chastity: "Religious thereby give witness to all Christ's faithful of that wondrous marriage between the Church and Christ her only spouse, a union which has been established by God and will be fully manifested on the world to come."[30] Professed religious, whose lives are patterned "after the manner of virginal and humble life, which Christ the Lord elected for Himself, and which His Virgin Mother also chose,"[31] are better signs of the undying fidelity and

---

29 *LG* §44 (74).

30 *PC* §12 (474). *VC* §34 (57) states: "In the consecrated life, particular importance attaches to the spousal meaning, which recalls the Church's duty to be completely and exclusively devoted to her Spouse, from whom she receives every good thing. This spousal dimension, which is a part of all consecrated life, has a particular meaning for women, who find therein their feminine identity and as it were discover the special genius of their relationship with the Lord." It also notes the spiritual character of this spousal relationship at *VC* §32 (32), where the "*objective superiority*" (emphasis in the text) of consecrated life is mentioned: "The consecrated life proclaims and in a certain way anticipates the future age, when the fullness of the Kingdom of heaven, already present in its first fruits and in mystery, will be achieved, and with the children of the resurrection will take neither wife nor husband, but will be like the angels of God (cf. *Mt* 22:30)."

31 *LG* §46 (77).

dedication of marriage—the marriage of Christ to his Church—than the marriages of married people.[32]

This fact indicates the complex and sophisticated pattern of analogy and equivocation needed to express adequately the nature of religious life as it models and enacts the spousal love of Christ for his Church, which itself involves a complex equivocal semantics relating the meaning of Christ and his Church, as spouses, to the meaning of human marriage. The concrete nature of earthly human marriage in all its dimensions, including physical, psychological, and cultural ones, supplies one baseline of meaning for the whole interplay of meanings. The specific spiritual character of the marriage of Christ to his bride the Church, which as incarnational embraces the physical, supplies the other baseline of meaning. Keeping the whole array in mind, as each semantic part plays its role, is the challenge. We need to ponder this complex semantic interplay and attempt to draw practical conclusions from the fact that religious life signifies a marriage and that the marriages present in the world have meaning that informs and articulates, in part, the meaning of religious life.

This complex array of equivocal signification regarding marriage is not a matter merely of inspirational and high-sounding ideas, abstractions, or theory. It is a matter of expressing the realities accurately. Thus, our connection through reflection and understanding to the reality of religious life, as it is and as it should be, is enhanced by appreciating and exploring the role that the full material meaning of ordinary marriage plays in the distinct but related meaning of religious life.

This point brings the two paradoxes of this paper together. The first paradox about the built-in tendencies in the structures and practices of religious life toward corruption apart from a fullness of

32   The documents, of course, recognize that Christian marriage is a sign of Christ's spousal love of the church. *LG* §41 (69), e.g., states how "married couples and Christian parents . . . can offer all men an example of unwearying and generous love, build up the brotherhood of charity, and stand as witnesses to and cooperators in the fruitfulness of Holy Mother Church. By such lives, they signify and share in that very love with which Christ loved his Bride and because of which he delivered Himself up on her behalf."

grace can find a partial effective remedy by applying deliberately to actual religious life the full material meaning of ordinary marriage. Reflection on ordinary married life can clarify the proper and specific meaning of religious life itself as a sign and living out already in the present age of the marriage of Christ and his Church.[33] This Church exercise, if itself performed under the influence of grace, which works in the particulars of life, has the potential to inform and stamp the operating understanding of religious life in a way that can encourage effective renewal through concrete acts of love. The second paradox regarding the complex equivocity of marriage in the meaning of religious life provides the conceptual warrant for the feasibility of the project.

By "the full material meaning of ordinary marriage" as the one baseline meaning for the spousal character of consecrated life, I have in mind a whole range of conditions and circumstances normally constituting family life, which give it its specific texture and tone, and provide it with its characteristic joys and challenges. This includes physical closeness and intimacy between family members and a relative inescapability of the demands of love, including cooperation in the maintenance of the home, caring and concern for spouses and children around-the-clock, and so on. This range of conditions and circumstances with their attendant responsibilities and expectations normal to marriage and family life in ordinary and human ways tends to build love and bring maturity to family members, both spouses and children. There is no claim here of perfection of love in normal marriage and family life. The "vocations crisis" in marriage, as measured merely by high divorce rates and broken homes among couples married in the Church apart from any gauge of seriously dysfunctional marriages, rivals in its own way the vocations problems in religious life. What I am trying to describe, nonetheless, is real and observable in countless families in their daily lives, despite being lived imperfectly. What I am trying to describe, indeed, is an arena of imperfect, but genuine, love, whose dynamics demand with

33 That the spousal meaning in consecrated life is meant in tangible and genuine ways, and not just as an idea or ideal, is indicated by VC §34 (57), which relates this matter in particular to women religious.

relative immediacy and concreteness, and also regularly elicit more or less successfully, responsible, and loving behavior and growth in marriage and family life.[34]

The deliberate and developed appropriate application of the meaning of ordinary married and family life to religious life for the sake of inspiring heightened love as an engine of renewal does not entail abandoning or substituting any of the distinctive structures, conditions, and circumstances of consecrated life, for activities necessary and common to ordinary family life. It is rather a matter of the living of religious life in a manner informed and stamped by the concrete and inescapable imperatives of love that show themselves tangibly and almost automatically in married and family life. For example, religious should genuinely love the people whom they serve, whether in active apostolates or at a physical distance by strictly spiritual means such as prayer, with the force of love that family members feel when bound by marriage, blood, and adoption.[35]

Our documents lay great stress on cooperation within community life for effective renewal of religious life. *Perfectae Caritatis* states unequivocally, "Successful renewal and proper adaptation cannot be achieved unless every member of a community cooperates." Beyond cooperation, when God's love is present "a religious community is a true family gathered in the Lord's name and rejoicing in his presence."[36] *Vita Consecrata* quotes Paul VI's encyclical letter *Ecclesiam Suam* that "dialogue is the new name of charity" and

34   One of my favorite examples of this dynamic is witnessing the transformation of students I have known from their university days until after a few years of assuming the responsibilities of marriage and family. This transformation is remarkable, especially in the case of some men.

35   Saint John Bosco in a letter writes: "First of all, if we wish to appear concerned about the true happiness of our foster children and if we would move them to fulfill their duties, you must never forget that you are taking the place of the parents of these beloved young people. I have always labored lovingly for them, and carried out my priestly duties with zeal. And the whole Salesian society has done this with me. . . . Let us regard these boys over whom we have some authority as our own sons. Let us place ourselves in their service. Let us be ashamed to assume an attitude of superiority. Let us not rule over them except for the purpose of serving them better." Quoted from the Office of Readings for January 31 in *The Liturgy of the Hours According to the Roman Rite*, vol. 3: *Ordinary Time, Weeks 1–17* (New York: Catholic Book Publishing, 1975), 1338.

36   *PC* §4 (469); §15 (477).

adds that the "consecrated life, by the fact that it promotes the value of fraternal life, provides a privileged experience of dialogue."[37] The increasingly complex relationships of cooperation, friendship, and true family—in religious life, as in all life—require reciprocity and mutual regard. In married life, so long as one partner shuts down or backs out, there is no recourse. In normal married life partners cannot get too far away from each other physically or emotionally, which does not always make life easy but makes cooperation, dialogue, and mutual assistance a daily and inescapable reality unless there is massive breakdown in the marriage. In a similar way, child-rearing, which parents frequently describe as the most difficult task of life, requires the personal mutual engagement with offspring. Cooperation, friendship, genuine family life in religious communities, where individuals are called together by God's choice rather than through the agency of romance, blood, or adoption, nevertheless need the same level of loving reciprocity forged in the demands of daily life for constant renewal of life and especially for meeting the challenges of adaptation to new conditions. The first paradox shows itself again in this situation. The bonds of communal life, as spiritual bonds depending on grace to thrive, can without an abundance of grace be less than what they should be, even in the natural order. Efforts by individuals to effect reform within established communities, however correct and well-meaning, can be counterproductive, unless accompanied by uncommon gifts of sanctity, as with a holy founder. In the ordinary circumstances of religious life, the prospects for effective and shared efforts at ongoing renewal can be improved if the self-understanding of religious communities can be stamped by the features of required cooperation and loving reciprocity that typically mark family life.

Jordan of Saxony, who succeeded Saint Dominic as master of the Order, wrote to the entire Order in 1233:

> We say a lot, we do a lot, we endure a tremendous lot, which would make us so much richer in virtue, so much more fruitful in merit, if

---

37 VC §74 (134).

only charity abounded in our hearts, directing and ordering everything towards our proper goal, which is God. But as it is, our minds are too often occupied with futile thoughts, our feelings drawn by futile desires, we do not carry through to its end the sifting and purging of our hearts' purposes, so it is hardly surprising that we are so slow to accomplish anything, so sluggish is our ascent towards perfection.[38]

This essay makes a modest proposal to apply aspects of the normal conditions of the life of the lay faithful, particularly those who are married and raising children, to the analysis of how to renew religious life. Such an analysis should bring a rededication and recommitment to living out in concrete and inescapable ways the loving practices that specifically constitute religious life, in analogy with daily inescapable ways that fill lay married and family life. In facing the challenges of contemporary renewal of religious life, Jordan's lament should be keenly felt. Why, with all the richness that constitutes both the meaning and the specific practices of consecrated life, is genuine contemporary renewal so elusive? The call to belong exclusively to Christ battles tendencies to belong merely to oneself. It does so through the love that pulls one out of oneself to Christ and to those for whom Christ died. This essay has proposed one specific and practical way, it is hoped, to actualize love for the pressing needs of constant and contemporary renewal of religious life.

---

38   *Early Dominicans: Selected Writings,* ed. with introduction by Simon Tugwell, O.P. (New York: Paulist Press, 1982), 124.

Eight

The Consecrated Life

Witness to Destiny

HUGH CLEARY, C.S.C.

The consecrated life is a living treasure, a treasure of the heart, a treasure of God's reign. As such, it always maintains its essential character throughout the ages, yet it adapts and renews in tumultuous periods of Church history so as to remain a vibrant sign of God's Kingdom. In *Vita Consecrata* Pope John Paul II expressed clearly the essential character of the consecrated life in its primary role in service to the Church:

> It is the duty of the consecrated life to show that the incarnate Son of God is the eschatological goal toward which all things tend, the splendor before which every other light pales and the infinite beauty which alone can fully satisfy the human heart. In the consecrated life, then, it is not only a matter of following Christ with one's whole heart . . . but of living and expressing this by conforming one's whole existence to Christ in an all encompassing commitment which foreshadows the eschatological perfection to the extent that this is possible in time.[1]

1 John Paul II, post-synodal apostolic exhortation *Vita Consecrata* (March 25, 1996), 1.

It seems evident that our present epoch is a tumultuous moment in the long tradition of the Christian community. This time, however, has the potential of seeing a vibrant renewal of the consecrated life through the transforming grace inherent in periods of crisis. It is our responsibility to assure the core identity and role of the consecrated life within the Church while it adapts to the particular needs of these times.

These present times are in large measure born of the eighteenth-century Age of Enlightenment, inaugurating a highly secular epoch. Some historians have characterized the French Revolution as a struggle for the life and death of Christianity, exalting freedom and reason over and against a belief in the very existence of God and the ethic of Divine Love. The impact of this secular age is wide and far, strong and pervasive.

Against this tide the essence of the consecrated life's meaning remains. Religious are the Church's countersign to the secular tenet that human life's final and ultimate end is nothing more and nothing less than death itself. Today the consecrated life stands in contradiction to the current scientific judgment that social and biological determinism represent the ultimate laws of existence. Religious are made of matter, but they are spirit as well.

Christian faith denies death's finality. We believe in the providence of God's love, a love that is eternal. We believe that we are made in the image and likeness of God's love; this truth is revealed through Old Testament Scriptures, through the incarnate Christ, and in the endless restlessness of our hearts. In this secular epoch religious have embarked on a renewal to strengthen their voice and the influence of their lives so as to stand in contradiction to the culture of death and proclaim the truth of God's reign of love in which they live and move and have their very being. Their vocation is a treasure of the Church.

The sources of this treasure's renewal in our time are numerous. Vatican II's *Lumen Gentium* and *Perfectae Caritatis* are two. Pope John Paul II's March 25, 1984, apostolic exhortation, *Redemptionis Donum* and his March 25, 1996, landmark encyclical *Vita Consecrata* are additional invaluable sources of renewal for the consecrated life. The Congregation for Institutes of Consecrated Life and Societies of Apostolic Life has also offered the Church ongoing sources of reflection for the renewal of the consecrated life. These feature Cardinal Somalo's instruction "Starting Afresh from Christ: A Renewed Commitment to Consecrated Life in the Third Millennium" and, on the occasion of the fortieth anniversary of *Perfectae Caritatis,* a comprehensive symposium aimed at revitalizing consecrated religious life as a faithful "witness of God's transfiguring presence," hosted by Cardinal Franc Rodé. His recent instruction "The Service of Authority and Obedience" is helpful and challenging.

International and local conferences of major superiors of religious institutes have assembled frequently to discuss pressing concerns of life and ministry. Numerous theologians have written extensively on the renewal of the consecrated life. Scores of consecrated religious have reflected deeply and written expansively on the objective meaning of the evangelical counsels while also enumerating the subjective characteristics of their particular community's founding charisms.

Most of these documents, if not all, situate the foundational meaning of the consecrated life within its classical purpose: we are first and foremost an eschatological sign for the present world of a new heaven and earth to come (Rv 21:1). It is impossible to comment on so many sources of renewal in one essay. Therefore, I restrict myself to three references that, though not all addressing the nature of the consecrated life directly, nevertheless when taken together provide fresh insight into the traditional formulation of the evangelical counsels. First, I will refer to *Spe Salvi.* Pope Benedict gives us a profound reflection on the present and future reality of God's reign, thereby broadening our appreciation for the consecrated life's eschatological witness. Second, I will highlight one of Benedict XVI's pertinent insights on the discipline of love, as expressed in his first encyclical, *Deus Caritas Est.* Third, I will offer an application of that particular insight through a short meditation on virtue by the founder of the Congregation of Holy Cross, Blessed Basile Moreau, who was beatified on September 15, 2007, an event that has proven to be a blessing beyond measure for the renewal of my own congregation.

The theology of eschatology refers to the eternal destiny of all human beings made in the image and likeness of God's love. The consecrated life is a visible sign of hope for the coming of that future. In *Spe Salvi,* the Holy Father asks the most pertinent question of eschatology: "Eternal life—what is it?"[2] Eternal life, he asserts, is not something interminable, an unending succession of days in the calendar, but rather, it is a mode of being, as expressed through a mystical encounter with Christ, both within time and beyond time. We thus know beyond the shadow of a doubt that Love's promise is fulfilled now and forever. It is like a supreme moment of joy "in which totality embraces us and we embrace totality."[3]

Eternal life—What is it? Jesus himself tells us in his prayer at the Last Supper:

> Father the hour has come. Give glory to your son, so that your son may glorify you, just as you gave him authority over all people, so that he may give eternal life to all you gave him. Now this is eternal life, that they should know you, the only true God, and the one whom you sent, Jesus Christ. I glorified you on earth by accomplishing the work that you gave me to do. Now glorify me, Father, with you, with the glory that I had with you before the world began. (Jn 17:1–5)

Jesus is the incarnation of God's love; he embodies the eschatological goal of perfect love to which all things tend. He makes visible the invisible God. Eternal life is an encounter with Christ, God's perfect love. It is a mystical encounter to which no other relationship compares yet which, paradoxically, imbues all other human relationships with the beauty and brilliance of Divine Love.

The publication in 2007 of the private writings of Mother Teresa of Calcutta illustrates this sense of eternal life. Much has been made of Mother Teresa's intense, decisive, though never to be repeated again, mystical encounter with Christ. It was a moment in time and beyond time. From that point on she was to encounter Christ daily in the poor and suffering of this world but never again in the intensity of that mystical moment.[4]

---

2   Benedict XVI, encyclical letter *Spe Salvi* (November 30, 2007), 10.
3   Ibid., 12.
4   Brian Kolodiejchuk, *The Private Writings of the "Saint of Calcutta"* (New York: Doubleday, 2007).

It seems that to some degree every consecrated religious has shared in that same experience. One's encounter with Christ is the primary source of this vocation. Religious are thus "witnesses of God's transfiguring presence."[5]

The consecrated life is a mode of Christ's presence within the Church and the world in the non-sacramental sign of community life, however frail and imperfect religious may be. Religious are all sinners striving to be saints, actively expressing Christ's self-giving, forgiving love, embodying and mirroring to the world here and now the eternal destiny that is ours. Within the witness of their own interpersonal relationships in community and congregational life, consecrated religious bear the heavy weight of giving testimony to an expression of God's eternal love. It is our vocation as consecrated religious, as an ecclesial community of believers, to make the eternal Christ visible to our world in a tangible, viable expression of love's promise of perfection, frail and sinful though we may be.

Eternal life is an expansive mode of living that knows no bounds, no distinctions. As Jesus answered the Scribes who tested his belief in an afterlife, many of us can also be quite mistaken in our understanding of the nature of eternal life. In the resurrection of the dead, he told them, we are like angels in Heaven; there is neither marrying nor giving in marriage (Mk 12:18–27). In this mode of being we no longer experience distinctions among us: there are no haughty comparisons, no social status, and no discrimination. Unique though we are, we are all in all, in the embrace of God's Love. "There is neither Jew nor Greek, there is neither slave nor free person, there is not male or female; for you are all one in Christ Jesus" (Gal 3:28). Eternal life begins in time when human beings welcome God's eternal love, finding expression in a willing sacrifice of self for others, in relationships that go beyond any measure of fair trade, balanced exchange, or mutual satisfaction.

The ecclesial community formed through consecrated life is united in this bond of God's love. We commit ourselves to each other, however imperfectly, not through a taking or losing of what

5   *Vita Consecrata*, 1.

is yours and what is mine, but through a love that is of God's posses-
sion, freely given, a love that will bow on bended knee to wash the
feet of friends, strangers, and enemies alike; a love that will sacrifice
everything so that others might live. It is a love that is untouched by
death, woven into the eternal destiny of God's creation. The time-
lessness of love has been placed in our hearts. It is this love that is
the treasure beyond price. In this mode of living there is no anxious
worry, no fear, no boredom, no amassing possessions, no power
over others, no lies, no bitterness, no jealousy, no hate.

Religious are far from perfect in living love of this eternal nature.
Sometimes sins and failures can seem an overpowering countersign
to what it is religious espouse, but forgiveness is of this eternal love.
Forgiveness is essential when one fails, falters, or sins. Jesus shed his
blood so that sin might be forgiven. When religious form this ecclesial mode of being, this community, they are an eschatological sign
of a new heaven and a new earth, where nothing can separate them
from God's love, not even death itself.

Love is complex. Divine Love at times seems the hardest love of
all to make personal. In his first encyclical, *Deus Caritas Est,* Pope
Benedict XVI clearly puts forward love's complexity, stating that
though there are many forms and facets of love, basically they are
in fact one single reality. Three Greek words, *eros, philia,* and *agape,*
express the many dimensions of love.[6]

Integrating these dimensions and living them as a single reality is the task of a lifetime. Pope Benedict asserts, "Love is indeed
'ecstasy' but not in the sense of a moment of intoxication, rather as
a journey, an ongoing exodus out of the closed inward-looking self
towards its liberation through self-giving, and thus towards authentic self-discovery and indeed the discovery of God."[7]

It is this kind of ecstasy that the consecrated life seeks to teach
and proclaim: the liberation of self gained through self-forgetting
love. It is life's supreme truth. This exodus journey out of the closed-
inward-looking self into an ecstatic self-giving love is a risky busi-

6   Pope Benedict XVI, encyclical letter *Deus Caritas Est* (December 25, 2005), 3.
7   Ibid., 6.

ness and seemingly foolhardy adventure. But the foolishness is of God! (Cf. 1 Cor 1:25.) Pope Benedict wisely counsels, "Eros needs to be disciplined and purified if it is to provide not just fleeting pleasure, but a certain foretaste of the pinnacle of our existence, of that beatitude for which our whole being yearns."[8] If consecrated religious are to give the world this foretaste of the pinnacle of our existence, they need to embody in their community life a passionate expression of love's supreme value beyond any other. The passion of *eros* requires a purified and disciplined integration with the self-giving *agape*. This love will then be a kind of primary, spontaneous instinct—intrinsic to our community's life-giving relationships.

How is this discipline and purification achieved? Love's passion seems best disciplined through the development and promotion of personal and communal virtues. Blessed Basile Moreau taught his religious that "a principal end of the Incarnation was to provide us with a Teacher, a Master and Model of all virtues."[9] Jesus is the model of all virtues. Virtues are key to appreciating the way in which religious embody and express their vows. The word "virtue" comes from the Latin *virtus,* meaning strength or power. Personalities of all people are formed by the constellation of strong and powerful virtues (and vices) that give us our identity. People know us through our personalities, through the way in which we present ourselves to them.

Virtues give a certain texture to human character and mark our way of being in the world. Our virtues and vices give coherence to this identity. They are living, breathing dispositions of our being that communicate to the world who we are and what values guide our lives. The theological virtues of faith, hope, and charity are gifts of God infused within us from our birth. They are part of our spiritual genetic structure. When we give them expression we strengthen them; when we neglect them they weaken and become barely discernible.

Religious can cultivate new virtues, adding them to the cluster

8 Ibid., 4.
9 Very Rev. Basile Moreau, "May 28th," in *Daily Meditations* (Washington, D.C.: Catholic Life Publications, 1958), 386.

of virtues that already define their character. The development and promotion of personal virtues are in fact the best means we have for disciplining love's passion. The so-called divine madness of *eros* seems capable of tearing us away from our finite existence toward an incomparable feeling of supreme happiness, but it quickly proves untrue without an effective discipline to help us, with grace, move beyond our own self-interest. When self-satisfaction and self-interest prove to be the object of our passionate concerns, we are sadly mistaken about the veracity of true love. It is only when love focuses on the good of others, whether the beloved or the stranger or the enemy, more than on our own personal interest, pleasure, or satisfaction, that we come to find love revealed in its truest and fullest expression.

Jesus, the incarnation, the embodiment of eternal love, reveals our more-than-empirical human destiny. The secular culture demands concrete proof that the absolute value of self-emptying love is the supreme experience of human life. If God's reign of eternal love is to be accepted by this skeptical epoch, believers need to validate this truth through concrete, measurable proofs just as Jesus glorified God by accomplishing the work that was given him.

Blessed Basile Moreau based the spirituality of his community, the Congregation of Holy Cross, on the Sulpician practice of conforming lives to Christ's life, so that through us, despite our human frailty, we might become, as individuals and as a community, a real and visible presence of Christ's self-forgetting love, thereby embodying here and now the gift of eternal life. Over the centuries it seems that one of the best ways Christian tradition has found to discipline love is to focus and manifest its power and passion through virtuous habits of the heart, which give love its visible form and expression.

As Jesus of Nazareth grew in wisdom and grace, he cultivated and acquired certain virtues in his life that gave form to his basic character, his personality, and his way of being. Jesus' virtuous living of chastity brought him to the desert wilderness, to the lonely mountain, and to the garden of Gethsemane, where he prayed with all his heart. Chastity committed Jesus to single-hearted intimacy with God, dispelling any temptation to live for himself. He was gentle and humble of heart. In the purity of his heart, Jesus and the Father were one. Sending us his Spirit, he invites us to be one with the triune God in the purity of our hearts. He illustrated this intimacy so beautifully in the image of the vine and the branches.

The purity of Jesus' undivided heart allowed him to mature in his virtuous living of obedience. Jesus' obedience, formed through chastity's prayerful intimacy with God, allowed him to unite his will with that of the Father. God wills that we love all people, without exception: the beloved, yes, of course, but so too all our family members, our neighbors, the stranger and the foreigner as well, and most terrifying of all, our enemy, such a harsh and dreadful love it is. "Do to others as you would have them do to you. For if you love only those who love you, what merit is there in that?" (Lk 6:29–30.)

Jesus taught us to be obedient: "This is my commandment: love one another as I love you. No one has greater love than this, to lay down one's love for one's friends" (Jn 15:12–13). In uniting his will with the Father's in perfect obedience Jesus could not but help to grow in the virtue of poverty.

Jesus' virtuous living of poverty afforded him such trusting dependence upon God's providing for him that he could exhaust himself freely sharing with his followers all that was in his heart, all the hours of his day. Forgetting himself, Jesus had pity on the vast crowds. He taught from the depth of his being, shared his life as a friend, and held nothing back. He lived in the fullness of God's Spirit, and he gave of himself completely, the very breath of his Spirit, until all was consummated. He exhorts us not to worry about preserving our lives because then, paradoxically, we will find that we are losing them. "Whoever seeks to preserve his life will lose it, but whoever loses his life will save it" (Lk 17:33).

Jesus' chastity, obedience, and poverty united as a single reality. The many and varied virtues he cultivated were manifestations of the one love, bringing us to our eternal destiny in God's being, "all in all."[10] Through these three virtues, these three schools of love,

10 Pope Benedict XVI [Joseph Cardinal Ratzinger], *God Is Near Us* (San Francisco: Ignatius Press, 2003), 145.

these three evangelical counsels, Jesus embodied God's eternal love.

Blessed Basile Moreau exhorted his religious to be in awe before the magnificence of their vocation:

> You are going to put on the mind and heart of the Master; you are going to reproduce in yourself his thoughts, his sentiments, his desires, his words and his actions; in short his entire way of life as it applies to your vocation. Your conscience will be your witness in the words of the apostle to the nations: "I live but it is no longer I who live but Christ who lives in me"; Jesus Christ speaks through my mouth, prays through my lips and acts through my body.[11]

Moreau's empirical approach is in tune with John Paul II's contention that consecrated religious best express their unique vocation by completely conforming themselves to Christ as individuals and as a community. As John the Evangelist stated so boldly: "We can be sure we are in God only when the one who claims to be living in him is living the same kind of life Christ lived" (1 Jn 2:6).

Consecrated religious seek to identify themselves so intimately with Jesus that through them the human family will see God made visible in their time and place, much as Jesus made visible the invisible God in his time and place. In our day we consider the world a global village. International religious congregations now have the extraordinary opportunity to witness in a privileged, unparalleled way a global sign of the new heaven and the new earth of God's reign.

My religious congregation is an illustrative example. Although an American citizen, I share a culture of life with my brothers from the Asian countries of Bangladesh, India, and the Philippines, with confreres from the African countries of Ghana, Uganda, Kenya, and Tanzania, with my brothers from the Latin American nations of Chile, Brazil, Peru, Mexico, and Haiti, with my brothers from the European nations of Italy, Ireland, and France, as well as my brothers from North America in Canada and the United States. Thus my citizenship is that of Heaven not simply that of earth. In God's love we are one.

---

11   Very Rev. Basile Moreau, C.S.C., "Sermon during Reception Ceremony of Carmelites—1856," in *Sermons* (unpublished collection compiled by Brother Joel Giallanza, C.S.C.).

We are responsible for each other. What is theirs is mine; what is mine is theirs. It is a quite remarkable witness, unlike any other. Clearly it is an extraordinary sign in time to the new heaven and new earth in eternity.

Pope Benedict describes well this important aspect of love:

> God's Kingdom is not an imaginary hereafter, situated in a future that will never arrive; his Kingdom is present wherever he is loved and wherever his love reaches us. His love alone gives us the possibility of soberly persevering day by day, without ceasing to be spurred on by hope, in a world which by its very nature is imperfect. At the same time his love is our guarantee of the existence of what we only vaguely sense and which nevertheless, in our deepest self, we await: a life that is "truly" life.[12]

Consecrated religious are a reflection of human destiny, a mirror to the world. We are also the human family of every age and time. We belong to one another; we are responsible for one another. There are no exceptions. We must live our vows in such a way that our witness will give hope to all not only to live in Christ but to die with him as well. In this way, and in this way only, his love will be our own.

Blessed Moreau chose as the motto for his congregation the verse *O Crux Ave, Spes Unica!* (Hail O Cross, Our Only Hope!), believing beyond any shadow of a doubt that the self-emptying asceticism of Christ's cross would reveal the fullness of love's promise. The consecrated life is a living treasure, a treasure of the heart; a treasure of God's Reign. How blessed those who have heard Jesus calling us: "Come. Follow me." How blessed we are to follow him!

12   *Spe Salvi*, 31.

Bibliography

Abbott, Walter M., S.J., ed. *The Documents of Vatican II: All Sixteen Official Texts Promulgated by the Ecumenical Council 1963–1965 Translated from the Latin.* London: Geoffrey Chapman, 1966.

Acta Synodalia Sacrosancti Concilii Oecumenici Vaticani II. Vatican City. Typis Polyglotis, 1983.

Alberigo, Giueseppe. *History of Vatican II.* Edited by Joseph Komonchak. 5 vols. Maryknoll, N.Y.: Orbis Press, 1995–2005.

Alvarez, Jean. "Focusing a Congregation's Future." *Human Development* 5 (Winter 1984): 25–34.

Augustine. *The Confessions.* Edited by Gillian Clark. Cambridge: Cambridge University Press, 1993.

———. *Tractates on the Gospel of John 28–54.* Fathers of the Church 88. Washington, D.C.: The Catholic University of America Press, 1993.

Balthasar, Hans Urs von, S.J. *The Christian State of Life.* San Francisco: Ignatius Press, 1983.

———. *Elucidations.* London: SPCK, 1971.

———. *Explorations in Theology I: The Word Made Flesh.* San Francisco: Ignatius Press, 1989.

———. *Explorations in Theology II.* San Francisco: Ignatius Press, 1991.

———. *The Glory of the Lord, V.* Edinburgh: T & T Clark, 1991.

———. *Heart of the World.* Translated by Erasmo Leiva. San Francisco: Ignatius Press, 1979.

———. *Love Alone Is Credible.* Translated by D. C. Schindler. San Francisco: Ignatius Press, 2004. Original German edition: *Glaubhaft is nur Liebe,* 1963.

———. *Prayer.* London: SPCK, 1975.

———. *Theo-Drama.* Vol. 2. San Francisco: Ignatius Press, 1990.

———. *Theo-Drama.* Vol. 4. San Francisco: Ignatius Press 1994.

————. *Therese of Lisieux: The Story of a Mission.* New York: Sheed and Ward, 1963.

Becker, Joseph M., S.J. *The Re-Formed Jesuits.* Vol. 1: *A History of Changes in Jesuit Formation during the Decade 1965–1975.* San Francisco: Ignatius Press, 1992.

Benedict XVI. "Address to the Catholic Educators at Conference Hall of the Catholic University of America in Washington, D.C." April 17, 2008.

————. "Address to Superiors General of the Institutes of Consecrated Life and Societies of Apostolic Life." May 22, 2006.

————. "Address to Young People and Seminarians at Saint Joseph Seminary." Yonkers, New York, April 19, 2008.

————. "Christmas Greetings to the Members of the Roman Curia and Prelature." December 22, 2005.

————. *Deus Caritas Est* (encyclical letter). 2005.

————. *God and Man.* San Francisco: Ignatius Press, 2002.

————. *God Is Near Us.* San Francisco: Ignatius Press, 2003.

————. Regina Caeli (address). April 27, 2008.

————. *Spe Salvi* (encyclical letter). 2007.

Butler, Sara, M.S.B.T. "Women and the Church." In *Gift of the Church,* edited by Peter C. Phan, 415–33. Collegeville, Minn.: Liturgical Press, 2000.

Brink, Laurie, O.P. "A Marginal Life: Pursuing Holiness in the 21st Century." *Horizons* 33, no. 3 (Spring 2008): 4–9.

Carey, Ann. "In Focus: Women Religious." *Our Sunday Visitor* 96, no. 49 (April 6, 2008): 11–14.

————. *Sisters in Crisis: The Tragic Unraveling of Women's Religious Communities.* Huntington, Ind.: Our Sunday Visitor Press, 1997.

Catholic Church. *The Liturgy of the Hours according to the Roman Rite.* Vol. 3: *Ordinary Time, Weeks 1–17.* Vol. 4: *Ordinary Time, Weeks 18–34.* New York: Catholic Book Publishing, 1975.

Congregation for Institutes of Consecrated Life and Societies of Apostolic Life. "The Service of Authority and Obedience" (instruction). May 11, 2008.

The Constitutions of the Society of Jesus and Their Complementary Norms. St. Louis, Mo.: Institute of Jesuit Sources, 1996.

Cooper, John M., ed. *Plato, Complete Works.* Indianapolis: Hackett Publishing, 1997.

Couturier, David B., O.F.M., Cap. "Religious Life at a Crossroads." *Origins* 36, no. 12 (August 31, 2006): 181–88.

Crosby, Michael H., O.F.M., Cap. *Can Religious Life Be Prophetic?* New York: Crossroad, 2005.

Darcy, Catherine C., R.S.M. *The Institute of the Sisters of Mercy of the Americas: The Canonical Development of the Proposed Governance Model.* Lanham, Md.: University Press of America, 1993.

"A Doctrinal Note on the Book *Reframing Religious Life.*" http://www.ewtn.com.

Dulles, Avery, S.J.. "Nature, Mission, and Structure of the Church." In *Vatican II: Renewal within Tradition,* edited by Matthew L. Lamb and Matthew Levering, 3–36. Oxford: Oxford University Press, 2008.

———. "True and False Reform." *First Things* 135 (August/September 2003): 14–19.

Egan, Robert, S.J.. "Why Not? Scripture, History, and Women's Ordination." *Commonweal* 135, no. 7 (April 11, 2008): 17–23, 26–27.

"Fraternal Life in Community." *Origins* 23, no. 40 (March 24, 1994): 693, 695 712.

Gardner, Lucy, David Moss, Ben Quash, and Graham Ward. *Balthasar at the End of Modernity.* Edinburgh: T & T Clark, 1999.

Goulding, Gill, I.B.V.M.. *Creative Perseverance.* Ottawa: Novalis, 2003

Gottemoeller, Doris, R.S.M.. "Religious Life: Who Is Invited and to What?" *Origins* 26, no. 17 (October 10, 1996): 265–69.

Groeschel, Benedict, C.F.R. "The Life and Death of Religious Life." *First Things* 174 (June/July, 2007): 12–15.

Healy, Nicholas, and David Schindler. "For the Life of the World: Hans Urs von Balthasar on the Church as Eucharist." In *The Cambridge Companion to Hans Urs von Balthasar,* 51–63. Cambridge: Cambridge University Press, 2006.

Ignatius Loyola. *Saint Ignatius of Loyola: Personal Writings.* Translated with introduction and notes by Joseph Munitiz, S.J., and Philip Endean, S.J. London: Penguin Classics, 1996.

———. *The Spiritual Exercises.* Translated by George Ganss, S.J. Chicago: Loyola University Press, 1992.

An Invitation to Systems Thinking: An Opportunity to Act for Systemic Change. http://www.lcwr.org/lcwrprogramsresources/Systems Thinking Handbook.pdf.

John Paul II. *Familiaris Consortio* (apostolic exhortation). 1981.

———. *Mulieris Dignitatem* (apostolic letter). 1988.

———. *Redemptoris Missio* (encyclical letter). 1990.

———. *Vita Consecrata* (post-synodal apostolic exhortation). 1996.

Johnson, Elizabeth A., C.S.J. "Between the Times: Religious Life and the Postmodern Experience of God." *Review for Religious* 53, no. 1 (January–February 1994): 6–28.

Kelly, George A. *The Battle for the American Church.* Garden City, N.Y.:
Image Books, 1981.

Kolodiejchuk, Brian. *The Private Writings of the "Saint of Calcutta."* New
York: Doubleday, 2007.

Lehner, Francis C., O.P., ed. *Saint Dominic: Biographical Documents.* Washington, D.C.: Thomist Press, 1964.

Lonergan, Bernard, S.J.. "Theology and Man's Future." *A Second Collection.*
London: Darton, Longman, and Todd, 1974.

Loser, Werner, S.J. "The Ignatian Exercises in the Work of Hans Urs von
Balthasar." In *Hans Urs von Balthasar His Life and Work,* edited by
David Schindler, 103–20. San Francisco: Ignatius Press, 1991.

Lozano, Juan, C.M.F. *Discipleship: Towards an Understanding of Religious
Life.* Chicago: Claret Center for Resources in Spirituality, 1980.

Marchetto, Agostino. *Il Consilio Ecumeniso Vaticano II: Contrappanto per
la sua Storia.* Vatican City: Liberria Editriece Vaticano, 2005.

McCann, Patricia, R.S.M.. "Double Crossed or Not? A Reflection of Kenneth Brigg's Study of American Sisters." *America* 195, no. 11 (October
16, 2005): 14–16.

McCarthy, Timothy G. *The Catholic Tradition: The Church in the Twentieth
Century.* Rev. and expanded ed. Chicago: Loyola Press, 1998.

McClory, Robert. "Ecumenical Monastery in Wisconsin Charts a New
Way." *National Catholic Reporter* (August 17, 2007): 10–11.

McDonough, Elizabeth, O.P.. "Juridical Deconstruction of Religious Institutes." *Studia Canonica* 26 (1992): 307–41.

———. "The Sisters' Survey Revisited." *Review for Religious* 63, no. 4
(2004): 387–401.

McIntosh, Mark A. *Christology from Within.* Notre Dame, Ind.: University
of Notre Dame Press, 2000.

Modde, M. M., O.S.F. *A Canonical Study of the LCWR.* Washington, D.C.:
The Catholic University of America Press, 1977.

Molinari, Paul, S.J., and Peter Gumpbel, S.J. *Chapter VI of the Dogmatic
Constitution "Lumen Gentium" on Religious Life: The Doctrinal Content
in the Light of the Official Documents.* Milan: Ancora, 1987.

Moreau, Basile, C.S.C. *Daily Meditations.* Washington, D.C.: Catholic Life
Publications, 1958.

———. "Sermon during Reception Ceremony of Carmelites—1856." In *Sermons.* Unpublished collection compiled by Brother Joel Giallanza, C.S.C.

Morey, Melanie, and John J. Piderit, S.J. *Catholic Higher Education: A Culture in Crisis.* Oxford: Oxford University Press, 2006.

Muckenhirn, M. Charles Borromeo, C.S.C., ed. *The Changing Sister.* Notre
Dame, Ind.: Fides, 1965.

———. *The Implications of Renewal.* Notre Dame, Ind.: Fides, 1967.

Neal, Marie Augusta, S.N.D.deN. *Catholic Sisters in Transition.* Wilmington, Del.: Michael Glazier, 1984.

———. *From Nuns to Sisters.* Mystic, Conn.: Twenty-Third Publications, 1990.

———. *Values and Interests in Social Change.* Englewood Cliffs, N.J.: Prentice Hall, 1965.

Nygren, David J., C.M., and Miriam D. Ukeritis, C.S.J. *The Future of Religious Orders in the United States: Transformation and Commitment.* Westport, Conn.: Praeger, 1993.

O'Connor, David F., S.T. "Two Forms of Consecrated Life: Religious and Secular Institutes." *Review for Religious* 45 (March–April 1986): 205–19.

O'Donnell, John, S.J. *Hans Urs von Balthasar.* London: Geoffrey Chapman, 1992.

O'Malley, John, S.J. "Vatican II: Did Anything Happen." *Theological Studies* 67, no. 1 (2006): 3–33.

———. *What Happened at Vatican II?* Cambridge, Mass.: Harvard University Press, 2008.

O'Murchu, Diarmuid, M.S.C. *Consecrated Religious Life: The Changing Paradigms.* Maryknoll, N.Y.: Orbis Books, 2005.

Paul VI. *Evangelica Testificatio* (apostolic letter). 1972.

———. *Evangelii Nuntiandi* (apostolic exhortation). 1975.

Plato. *Complete Works,* edited with introduction and notes by John M. Cooper; translated by G. M. A. Grube. Indianapolis: Hackett Publishing, 1997.

Pontifical Council for Culture and Pontifical Council for Interreligious Dialogue. *Jesus Christ, the Bearer of the Water of Life: A Christian Reflection on the "New Age."* http://www.vatican.va/roman_curia/pontifical_councils/interelg/documents/rc_pc_interelg_doc_20030203_new-age_en.html.

Quash, Ben. "Ignatian Dramatics." *The Way* 38 (January 1988): 77–86.

———. "The Theo-Drama." In *The Cambridge Companion to Hans Urs von Balthasar,* edited by Edward T. Oakes and David Moss, 143–57. Cambridge: Cambridge University Press, 2004.

Quiñonez, Lora Ann, C.D.P., ed. *Starting Points: Six Essays Based on the Experience of U.S. Women Religious.* Washington, D.C.: Leadership Conference of Women Religious (LCWR), 1980.

Quiñonez, Lora Ann, C.D.P. and Mary Daniel Turner, S.N.D.deN. "From CMSW to LCWR: A Story of Birth and Transformation." *Review for Religious* 49 (1990): 295–302.

———. *The Transformation of American Catholic Sisters*. Philadelphia: Temple University Press, 1992.

Ratzinger, Joseph. *God and Man*. San Francisco: Ignatius Press, 2002.

Renewal through Community and Experimentation. Washington, D.C.: Canon Law Society of America, 1968.

Rousseau, Phillip. *Pachomius: The Making of a Community in Fourth-Century Egypt*. Transformation of the Classical Heritage 6. Berkeley: University of California Press, 1985.

Sabourin, Justine, R.S.M. *The Amalgamation: A History of the Union of the Religious Sisters of Mercy in the United States of America*. St. Meinrad, Ind.: Abbey Press, 1976.

Sacred Congregation for Bishops. *Directives for the Mutual Relations between Bishops and Religious in the Church "Mutuae Relationes."* 1978.

Sacred Congregation for Religious and Secular Institutes (SCRIS). "Essential Elements in the Church's Teaching on Religious Life as Applied to Institutes Dedicated to the Works of the Apostolate." *Origins* 13 (July 7, 1983): 18–22.

Schneiders, Sandra, I.H.M. *Beyond Patching: Faith and Feminism in the Catholic Church*. Mahwah, N.J.: Paulist Press, 1991.

———. *Finding the Treasure: Locating Catholic Religious Life in a New Ecclesial and Cultural Context*. Mahwah, N.J.: Paulist Press, 2000.

———. *New Wineskins: Re-imagining Religious Life Today*. Mahwah, N.J.: Paulist Press, 1986.

———. *Selling All: Commitment, Consecrated Celibacy, and Community in Catholic Religious Life*. Mahwah, N.J.: Paulist Press, 2001.

———. "There Is No Going Back: U.S. Women Religious Have Given Birth to a New Form of Religious Life." *National Catholic Reporter* 45, no. 11 (March 20, 2009): 12, 14.

Schüssler Fiorenza, Elisabeth. *Discipleship of Equals: A Critical Feminist Ekklesia-logy of Liberation*. New York: Crossroad, 1993.

"Starting Afresh from Christ: A Renewed Commitment to Consecrated Life in the Third Millennium." *Origins* 32 (July 4, 2002): 129, 131–48.

Trainor, Mary, R.S.M. "A Participative Approach to Corporate Restructuring in the World of Religious Women." Presented to the Conference on Coalitions at Boston University, May 1988.

Tugwell, Simon, O.P.. *Early Dominicans: Selected Writings*. New York: Paulist Press, 1982.

Wittberg, Patricia, S.C. *From Piety to Professionalism, and Back? Transformation of Organized Religious Virtuosity*. Lanham, Md.: Rowman and Littlefield, 2006.

World Synod of Bishops. *Justicia in Mund*. 1971.

Contributors

SARA BUTLER, M.S.B.T., is professor of dogmatic theology at the University of St. Mary of the Lakes, Mundelein, Illinois. She has been a consultant to the U.S. bishops since 1972, serves on two international ecumenical commissions (Anglican–Roman Catholic and Baptist–Catholic dialogues), and was a member of the International Theological Commission (as one of the first two women theologians appointed) from 2004 to 2009. She recently published *The Catholic Priesthood and Women: A Guide to the Teaching of the Church* (Chicago: Hillenbrand), and has written over fifty scholarly articles. During a term on the General Council of the Missionary Servants of the Most Blessed Trinity (1978–88) she worked on the revision of their constitutions and coauthored the *Rule of Life* shared by the Missionary Cenacle Family. Sister Sara is a member of the Academy of Catholic Theology, the Catholic Theological Society of America, and the Fellowship of Catholic Scholars.

HUGH CLEARY, C.S.C., is a priest in the Congregation of Holy Cross. He holds a PhD from Duquesne University in formative spirituality, a master's in counseling psychology from Loyola in Chicago, and a MTh from Notre Dame. Father Cleary was superior general of the Congregation 1998–2010, provincial of the Eastern Province of Priests of Brothers of Holy Cross, and novice master for the Congregation in the United States. He also participated in parochial work in Brooklyn and North Easton, Massachusetts.

GILL GOULDING C.J., is associate professor of systematic theology and spirituality at Regis College, the Jesuit Graduate School of Theology at the University of Toronto. She is also chair of the Theology Department of the Toronto School of Theology. Her research interests focus in the area of the Trinity and ecclesiology, the theology of Hans Urs von Balthasar, and the theology of the Spiritual Exercises of St. Ignatius Loyola. Her recent publications include: "The Cardoner Imperative," *The Way*, January 2009; "Glimpses of Glory," *Religious Life Review*, January/February 2009. She is currently [2009] on sabbatical in Ireland as the Veale Chair at Milltown Institute of Theology and Philosophy Dublin. She is writing in the area of ecclesiology a monograph provisionally titled "Ignatian Insights for an Insightful Church" and completing a work on the Trinity that she began while an International Visiting Fellow at the Woodstock Theological Center, Georgetown, Washington, D.C.

RICHARD GRIBBLE, C.S.C., a priest in the Congregation of Holy Cross, is a professor of Religious Studies at Stonehill College. He holds a doctorate in Church history from the Catholic University of America and an MDiv and STM from the Jesuit School of Theology in Berkeley, California. Previously he served in parish ministry in Arizona and as rector of Moreau Seminary at the University of Notre Dame. He has written four critical biographies, including *American Apostle of the Family Rosary: The Life of Patrick J. Peyton, CSC* and *An Archbishop for the People: The Life of Edward J. Hanna.* He has contributed essays to many journals, including *The Catholic Historical Review, American Catholic Studies,* and *The Journal of Church and State.*

JOSEPH T. LIENHARD, S.J., entered the Society of Jesus in 1958 and was ordained in 1971. He received the degree "Dr. theol." (doctor of theology) from the University of Freiburg (Germany) in 1975 with a dissertation on Paulinus of Nola and early Western monasticism and was granted the "Habilitation," or degree beyond the doctorate, by the same university in 1986 for a work on Marcellus of Ancyra. From 1975 to 1990 Fr. Lienhard taught at Marquette University and since 1990 he has taught at Fordham University. He has held visiting professorships at John Carroll University, Boston College, St. Joseph's Seminary (Dunwoodie), the Pontifical Biblical Institute, and the Pontifical Gregorian University. Since 1997 he has been the managing editor of *Traditio.* Fr. Lienhard is the author of four books and more than fifty scholarly articles. Among his books are *The Bible, the Church, and Authority: The Canon of the Christian Bible in History and Theology* (1995); *St. Joseph in Early Christianity: Devotion and Theology; A Study and an Anthology of Patristic Texts* (1999); and the translation *Origen: Homilies on Luke; Fragments on Luke* in the series Fathers of the Church (1996).

ELIZABETH MCDONOUGH, O.P., holds a JCD from the Catholic University of America and an STL from the Pontifical Faculty of the Immaculate Conception in Washington, D.C. Most recently she was Bishop James A. Griffin Professor of Canon Law at the Pontifical College Josephinum. Prior teaching included a position on the Pontifical Faculty of Canon Law at the

Catholic University of America and at Mount Saint Mary's Seminary. She has published in *The Antonianum, The Jurist, Canon Law Society of America Proceedings,* and *Studia Canonica* and has authored one book, several book chapters, and numerous encyclopedia entries. Since 1990, Sister Elizabeth has published one hundred successive Canonical Counsel essays in *Review for Religious.* She consults extensively for dioceses and religious communities in the United States and abroad. In 2006 she was awarded the *Pro Ecclesia et Pontifice Cross* by Pope Benedict XVI. She is a member of the Dominican Sisters of Our Lady of the Springs of Bridgeport (Conn.).

BISHOP ROBERT C. MORLINO is the fourth bishop of the Diocese of Madison. He was ordained to the priesthood in 1974 for the Maryland Province of the Society of Jesus. His education includes a master's degree in philosophy from the University of Notre Dame, the master of divinity degree from the Weston School of Theology in Cambridge, Massachusetts, and a doctorate in moral theology from the Gregorian University in Rome, with specialization in fundamental moral theology and bioethics. Before and after his incardination as a priest of the Diocese of Kalamazoo in 1981, Bishop Morlino taught philosophy and theology in numerous university settings. He was named bishop of Helena on July 6, 1999 and bishop of Madison on May 23, 2003. Since 2005, Bishop Morlino has served as chairman of the board of directors of the National Catholic Bioethics Center (NCBC), and in 2008, for his work in defense of the dignity of the human person, Bishop Morlino was awarded Human Life International's Cardinal von Galen Award. The same year, he received the St. Edmund's Medal of Honor, awarded to Catholics who have used their God-given talents in promoting the common good.

KURT PRITZL, O.P., died in February 2011. At the time of his death he was associate professor and dean of the School of Philosophy at the Catholic University of America. His initial appointment to the School of Philosophy was made in 1980, after doctoral studies concentrating in ancient Greek philosophy at the University of Toronto. He became dean of the school in 2000 after an international search, having served as acting and interim dean (1997–98, January 1999–2000). His scholarly work in Greek philosophy centers on the theory of knowledge and accounts of the soul, with publications primarily on the thought of the pre-Socratic thinkers and Aristotle. His recent publications include "The Place of Intellect in Aristotle," from a plenary address at the American Catholic Philosophical Association Annual Meeting on "Intelligence and the Philosophy of Mind," and the introduction and introductory essay in the forthcoming collection of essays

"Truth: Studies of a Robust Presence," which Father Pritzl is editing. He has also published on the role of philosophy in priestly formation. Father Pritzl is a member of the Province of Saint Joseph of the Order of Preachers, more commonly known as the Dominican Order.

CARDINAL FRANC RODÉ, C.M., was born in Ljubljana, Slovenia. In 1945 he fled with his family from Rodica by Domžale to Austria and then later emigrated to Argentina. He was ordained for the Vincentians in 1960 and holds a doctorate in theology from the Catholic Institute of Paris. He returned to Slovenia in 1965 and served as curate in Celje and Šentjakob ob Savi. He was also director of the Vincentian scholasticate and provincial visitator. At the same time he taught fundamental theology and missiology at the Theological Faculty of Ljubljana. He became an official at the Secretariat for Non-Believers in 1981 and its undersecretary the following year. In 1993 he was named secretary of the Pontifical Council for Culture. On March 5, 1997, Pope John Paul II appointed him archbishop of Ljubljana. On February 11, 2004, he was appointed prefect of the Congregation for Institutes of Consecrated Life and Societies of Apostolic Life. On March 24, 2006, His Holiness Pope Bendedict XVI elevated him to Cardinal. Today he holds emeritus status in the Curia.

Index

Abortion, 52n34, 55, 68

Acta Synodalia, 78–80

Agape, 149–50. *See also* Love

Aggiornamento, 6, 28

Alberigo, Giuseppe, 5

Antony, St., 3, 93

Apophthegmata patrum (Sayings of the Desert Fathers), 93

Apostolic religious life. *See* Religious life

Apostolic visitation, 62, 68n1

Aquinas, 131

Aristotle, 131

Asceticism, 30, 48, 51, 93, 118. *See also* Monasticism

Augustine of Hippo, St., 95, 98

Balthasar, Hans Urs von, S.J., 14, 111–14, 116–25

Basil of Caesarea, St., 95

Benedict XVI, Pope, 13, 15, 29, 33, 37, 40, 102; *Deus Caritas Est*, 113, 146, 149–50; hermeneutic of continuity, 11, 35; hermeneutic of discontinuity, 11, 24–26; Spe Salvi, 146, 147; visit to U.S. (2008), 20–22

Benedictines, 95, 97

Boff, Leonardo, 55

Bologna School, 5

Butler, Sara, M.S.B.T., 12, 112

Cabrini, Frances Xavier, St., 21

Capuchins, 4

Carey, Ann, 9

Carmelites, 97

Carthusians, 91–92, 94, 100

Catechesis, 37–39

Celibacy. *See* Chastity

Charism: commitment to founder's, 4, 9, 12, 14, 20, 35–36, 49, 64–66; contribution to renewal, 38–39; fidelity to, 30, 37; present state of, 22–23, 30, 49

Charity, 14, 38, 45, 64–65, 79, 127–29, 150

Charlemagne, 95

Chastity: adaptation to lifestyle, 48–51; and celibacy, 137–38; deconstruction of, 104–6; of Jesus, 151–52; meaning of, 47; vows of, 13–14, 33, 41, 65, 78–83

Christian State of Life, The (Balthasar), 113

Church and the Second Sex, The (Daly), 71

CICLSAL. *See* Congregation for Institutes of Consecrated Life and Societies of Apostolic Life

Cistercians, 95, 97

Civil rights movement, 51, 54. *See also* Social justice

Cleary, Hugh, C.S.C., 14–15

Hamer, Cardinal Jean Jérôme, 68
Healy, Nicholas, 124
Heidegger, Martin, 113
Hermeneutics: of continuity and reform, 7, 11, 15, 31–36, 107; of discontinuity and rupture, 7, 11, 15, 24–30, 102, 107
Hobbes, Thomas, 131
Holy Spirit, 20, 30, 31, 34, 41, 46, 65, 74
Humanae Vitae (1968), 6, 54, 55, 103–4

Ignatius of Loyola, St., 101–2, 117, 119–20, 121–23. *See also writings by title*
Imbelli, Robert, 5
Institute for Forgiveness, University of Wisconsin, Madison, 106
Institute of the Sisters of Mercy of the Americas, 68n1, 69n2
Institutio Christiana, 88
Into Great Silence (film), 91–92

Jesuits, 21, 25n49, 80, 96, 97, 119, 126
Jesus Christ: as embodiment of eternal love, 111, 147, 151, 152; relationship with, 63–64; as spouse, 139–40; vows to, 14, 41–43, 44, 103–7
John, St. (apostle), 98, 122
John, St. (the Evangelist), 153
John Paul II, Pope, 19–20, 37, 46, 52, 132, 134, 144, 153
Johnson, Elizabeth A., C.S.J., 8
John XXIII, Pope, 31, 68
Jordan of Saxony, Bl., 142, 143
Joseph, Mother, Sisters of Providence, 21
Joy, 34–35, 106–7, 147
Justitia in mundo (Justice in the World, 1971), 52, 55n43

Kino, Father Eusebio, 21
Küng, Hans, 55

Language of God, 101–7
Leadership Conference of Women Religious (LCWR), 7, 8, 44, 62, 72–73, 76, 84–85, 86

Lex credendi, lex orandi, lex vivendi, 88
Liberation theology, 51, 54, 63, 105. *See also* Social justice
Lienhard, Joseph T., S.J., 13
Lonergan, Bernard, 116
Love: credibility of, 111–26; discipline of, 146, 149–51; Divine, 14, 119, 126, 135, 149; expressed in paschal mystery, 112, 115; language of, 126, 149–50; philosophical outlook of, 130–32; renewal of, 134–38
Lozano, Juan, C.M.F., 81
Lumen Gentium, 8, 13, 78–80, 127–28, 133, 137–38, 145

Magisterium, 11, 12, 28, 31, 57, 61, 79, 103
Maior dissimilitude, 121n23
Mansour, Agnes Mary, R.S.M., 86
Marchetto, Archbishop Agostino, 5
Marquette, Father Jacques, 21
Marriage: relation to religious life, 47, 135, 138–43; as sacrifice, 103, 104–5
Mary, Blessed Virgin, 121–22
Mary Magdalene, St., 122
Mater et Magistra (1961), 51n31
McCann, Patricia, R.S.M., 10
McCarthy, Timothy, 5
McDonough, Elizabeth, O.P., 12
Mendicant orders, 3, 89, 95–96
Mergers. *See* Reconfigurations
Monasticism, 3, 8, 48–51, 82, 93–95
Moreau, Blessed Basil Anthony Mary, C.S.C., 15, 146, 150, 151, 153, 154
Morlino, Bishop Robert, 13
Mulieris Dignitatem, 46n14

National Religious Retirement Office (NRRO), 69
Neal, Marie Augusta, S.N.D.deN., 84–85
Neumann, John, St., 21
New Wineskins (Schneiders), 8
New York Times, 55, 68, 86
Nietzsche, Friedrich Wilhelm, 131
Nygren-Ukeritis study (1993), 83n24

Obedience, 13–14, 118–19; change in order of vows, 78–83; and conscience, 104–5; instructions, 34–35; meaning of, 46–47
O Crux Ave, Spes Unica! (C.S.C. motto), 154
Octogesima adveniens (1971), 51n31
O'Donnell, John, S.J., 125
O'Malley, John W., S.J., 5–6
On Christianity and Social Progress (1961). *See Mater et Magistra*
On the Development of Peoples (1967). *See Populorum Progressio*
On the Dignity and Vocation of Women (1988). *See Mulieris Dignitatem*
On the Renewal of the Religious Life (1972). *See Evangelica Testificatio*
Order of Friars Minor, 4
Order of Friars Preachers, 129

Pacem in Terris, 51n31
Pachomius, St., 93–94
Parish Visitors of Mary Immaculate, New York, 96
Paschal mystery: love expressed in, 115–16
Pastoral Constitution on the Church in the Modern World (1965). *See Gaudium et Spes*
Paul, St. (Apostle), 23, 63, 103, 111, 115
Paul VI, Pope, 52, 63, 141
Perfectae Caritatis, 7, 9, 12, 14, 26–27, 32, 48, 65, 70, 74, 78, 80, 127, 129–30, 133, 136, 138, 141, 145, 146
Peter, St. (Apostle), 38, 122
Phaedo (Plato), 131
Philia, 149. *See also* Love
Plato, 131, 135
Polarization, 7, 12, 42–44, 57–59
Populorum Progressio, 51n31
Poverty, 13–14, 33, 41, 78–83, 136, 152; deconstruction of, 103–7; meaning and promise of, 47–48; in *Perfectae Caritatis,* 27; and self-surrender, 116; vows of, 78–83
Prayer: call to, 113, 114; in community,

30, 33, 49, 135; in the early Church, 93–94; as obedience, 103, 106; and the sacraments, 38
Priesthood. *See* Religious life
Pritzl, Kurt, O.P., 14
"Problem of socialism," 137
Pro-Life Sunday (Oct. 7, 1984), 68

Quinn Commission, 67n1, 72, 73n7, 77n15, 86, 87n32

Ratzinger, Joseph. *See* Benedict XVI
Reconfigurations, 69, 69n2, 73, 87
Redemptionis Donum (1984), 145
Redemptoris Missio (1990), 52n37
Regina Caeli, 22n4
Regula fidei, 88
Religious and Human Promotion (1978/80), 52n33
Religious life: competing "ecclesiologies," 54–57; elements of, 12, 24, 34–36, 49–51, 94–95; as gift, 41–42; history of, 3–4, 19–22, 93–97; integration of contemplation and action in, 119–21; landscape today, 7–10, 22–24; paradoxes of, 135–40; polarization of, 7, 12, 42–44, 57–59; progressive approach, 7–10, 11, 81–84, 85–89, 100; reforming of, 19–40, 99; relation to marriage, 47, 135, 138–43; relation to priesthood, 56, 125–26; renewal of, 5–14, 19–40, 64–66, 74–77, 92–99, 127–43; signs and symbols in, 92–100; as "treasure," 12, 15, 42–45, 63–66, 144–45, 154; and women, 48–49, 55–56, 67–70, 76, 81–83, 89
Re-novatio, 74–75
Ressourcement, 6
Rettig, John W., 98n3
Rodé, Cardinal Franc, C.M., 11, 12, 102, 146
Roman Curia. *See* Curia
Ruini, Camillo, 5
Rules for Thinking, Judging and Feeling with the Church (Ignatius), 121